MULTIPLICATION AND DIVISION WORD PROBLEMS: NO PROBLEM!

MATH BUSTERS WORD PROBLEMS

Rebecca Wingard-Nelson

NEED MORE PRACTICE?
Free worksheets available at
http://www.enslow.com

Enslow Publishers, Inc.
40 Industrial Road
Box 398
Berkeley Heights, NJ 07922
USA

http://www.enslow.com

Library of Congress Cataloging-in-Publication Data

Wingard-Nelson, Rebecca.
Multiplication and division word problems : no problem! / by Rebecca Wingard-Nelson.
    p. cm. — (Math busters word problems)
Summary: "Presents a step-by-step guide to understanding word problems with multiplication and
division"— Provided by publisher.
Includes bibliographical references and index.
ISBN 978-0-7660-3370-2
1. Multiplication—Juvenile literature. 2. Division—Juvenile literature. 3. Word problems
(Mathematics)—Juvenile literature. I. Title.
QA155.W7538 2011
513.2'13—dc22
                                        2009043926

Printed in the United States of America

062010 Lake Book Manufacturing, Inc., Melrose Park, IL

10 9 8 7 6 5 4 3 2 1

To Our Readers: We have done our best to make sure all Internet Addresses in this book were active and appropriate when we went to press. However, the author and the publisher have no control over and assume no liability for the material available on those Internet sites or on other Web sites they may link to. Any comments or suggestions can be sent by e-mail to comments@enslow.com or to the address on the back cover.

✪ Enslow Publishers, Inc., is committed to printing our books on recycled paper. The paper in every book contains 10% to 30% post-consumer waste (PCW). The cover board on the outside of each book contains 100% PCW. Our goal is to do our part to help young people and the environment too!

Photo credits: Shutterstock, pp. 5, 9, 11, 13, 14, 17, 18, 21, 22, 25, 26, 30, 33, 37, 38, 41, 43, 45, 47, 49, 50, 52, 54, 57, 61; © Comstock/PunchStock, pp. 7, 29, 35; © Digital Vision, p. 58.

Cover photo: © Luis Alvarez/iStockphoto.com

Free Worksheets are available for this book at http://www.enslow.com. Search on the *Math Busters Word Problems* series name. The publisher will provide access to the worksheets for five years from the book's first publication date.

Contents

Introduction

When you spend two hours playing twenty-eight online games, you're living in a word problem!
Math is everywhere; you just might not realize it all the time because math isn't always written as a math problem.

This book will help you understand how multiplication and division are used in word problems.
The step-by-step method can help students, parents, teachers, and tutors solve any word problem.
The book can be read from beginning to end or used to review a specific topic.

? ?
How do I start? What do I do if I get stuck? ?
What if the answer is wrong when I check it? ?
Word problems are hard for me!
? ?

Get Involved!

You can watch a swim meet and see swimmers racing across a pool, but if you want to *learn* to swim, you must get in the water. Solving math problems is not a spectator sport. You may first watch how others solve word problems, but then you need to solve them for yourself, too. Go ahead, jump in!

Practice!

Even the most gifted athlete or musician will tell you that in order to play well, you must practice. The more you practice anything, the better and faster you become at it. The same is true for problem solving. Homework problems and class work are your practice.

Learning Means <u>Not</u> Already Knowing!

If you already know everything, there is nothing left to learn. Every mistake you make is a potential learning experience. When you understand a problem and get the right answer the first time, good for you! When you do NOT understand a problem but figure it out, or you make a mistake and learn from it, AWESOME for you!

Questions, Questions!

Ask smart questions. Whoever is helping you does not know what you don't understand unless you tell them. You must ask a question before you can get an answer.

Ask questions early. Concepts in math build on each other. Today's material is essential for understanding tomorrow's.

Don't Give Up!

Stuck on homework? There are many resources for homework help.
• Check a textbook.
• Ask someone who does understand.
• Try looking up sources on the Internet (but don't get distracted).
• Read this book!

Getting frustrated? Take a break.
• Get a snack or a drink of water.
• Move around and get your blood flowing. Then come back and try again.

Stuck on a test? If you do get stuck on a problem, move on to the next one. Solve the problems you understand first. That way you won't miss the problems you do understand because you were stuck on one you didn't. If you have time, go back and try the ones you skipped.

Wrong answer? Check the math; it could be a simple mistake. Try solving the problem another way. There are many problem-solving strategies, and usually more than one of them will work. Don't give up. If you quit, you won't learn anything.

Problem-Solving Steps

What steps can I take to solve word problems? If I follow the steps, will I be more likely to get a correct answer? Will I have less trouble finding the answer?

Problem-Solving Steps

Step 1: Understand the problem.
Step 2: Make a plan.
Step 3: Follow the plan.
Step 4: Review.

Step 1: Understand the problem.

Read the problem. Read the problem again. This may seem obvious, but this step may be the most important.

Ask yourself questions like:

Do I understand all of the words in the problem?

Can I restate the problem in my own words?

Will a picture or diagram help me understand the problem?

What does the problem ask me to find or show?

What information do I need to solve the problem? Do I have all of the information I need?

Underlining the important information can help you to understand the problem. Read the problem as many times as it takes for you to have a clear sense of what happens in the problem and of what you are asked to find.

Step 2: Make a plan.

There are many ways to solve a math problem. Choosing a good plan becomes easier as you solve more problems. Some plans you may choose are:

Make a list.

Draw a picture.

Use logical reasoning.

Use mental math.

Use a model.

Write an equation.

Guess and check.

Work backward.

Solve a simpler problem.

Use a number line or graph.

Use a table.

Use a proportion.

Step 3: Follow the plan.

Now that you understand the problem and have decided how to solve it, you can carry out your plan. Use the plan you have chosen. If it does not work, go back to step 2 and choose a different plan.

Step 4: Review.

Look over the problem and your answer. Does the answer match the question? Does the answer make sense? Is it reasonable? Check the math. What plan worked or did not work? Looking back at what you have done on this problem will help you solve similar problems.

Brant's friends are spending Saturday at his house having a movie marathon. They rented 6 movies for $4 each. Each movie is about 2 hours long. How much did they pay to rent the movies?

Step 1: Understand the problem.

Read the problem. What does the problem ask you to find? **The amount Brant and his friends paid to rent the movies.**

What information do you need to solve the problem? **The cost to rent a movie and the number of movies that were rented.**

Is there extra information? **Yes. The problem tells you each movie is about 2 hours long. This information is not needed to solve the problem.**

Step 2: Make a plan.

This problem tells you that it cost $4 to rent each movie. Problems that tell you a value for one item, and ask you to find a value for more than one of the same item are multiplication problems. Problems that use words such as *each*, *every*, *of*, *per*, *rate*, *times*, and *multiple* may be multiplication problems.

Let's write an equation.

Step 3: Follow the plan.

Multiply the number of movies rented (6) by the cost of each rental ($4).

One way to write an equation is to write words first, then change the words to numbers and math symbols.

number of movies rented **times** **price per rental** **equals** **total cost**.

6 x $4 = $24

Brant's friends paid $24 to rent the movies.

Step 4: Review.

Does the answer match the question?
Yes. The problem asks for an amount of money.

Check the answer.
Multiplication problems can be checked using repeated addition. Add $4 for each movie the friends rented.

$4 + $4 + $4 + $4 + $4 + $4 = $24

Step 1: Understand the problem.

Read the problem. Restate the question in your own words.
What is the cost of unlimited text messaging for a year?

What does the problem ask you to find?
The amount Leah pays for text messaging for a year.

What information do you need to solve the problem?
The amount she pays each month, and the number of months.

Do you have all of the information that you need?
The problem does not tell you the number of months in a year. Sometimes you need additional information to solve a problem. There are 12 months in a year.

Step 2: Make a plan.

Each month for 12 months Leah pays $10. You can count by 10s to find the total for a year.

Step 3: Follow the plan.

Count by 10s until you have counted twelve 10s.

10, 20, 30, 40, 50, 60, 70, 80, 90, 100, 110, 120
  1   2   3   4   5   6   7   8   9   10 11 12

Leah pays $120 for a full year of text messaging.

Step 4: Review.

Does the answer match
the question?
**Yes, the problem asks
for a dollar amount.**

Does the answer make sense?
Yes.

Is there another way you
can solve this problem?
**Yes. The problem was
solved by counting by 10s.
Multiplication is a quick way
to count by the same number.
Since we need to know how
much twelve 10s are,
multiply.**

12 × 10 = 120

⑤ Draw a Picture

A vending machine package contains 6 small doughnuts. Matt ate 7 full packages. How many doughnuts did Matt eat?

Step 1: Understand the problem.

Read the problem. Is there anything you do not understand?

What does the problem ask you to find?
The number of doughnuts that Matt ate.

What information do you need to solve the problem? Is there extra information?
You need to know how many packages of doughnuts Matt ate, and how many doughnuts are in each package.

Step 2: Make a plan.

Let's draw a picture to understand what happens in the problem. Then write an equation that matches the drawing.

Step 3: Follow the plan.

Draw seven packages of doughnuts. Each package has six doughnuts. You can use dots or small circles for each doughnut.

If you do not recognize what operation happens in the problem, a drawing can help. This problem combines equal sets. It is a multiplication problem. Write a multiplication equation.

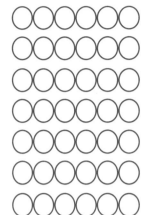

7 × 6 = 42

Matt ate 42 small doughnuts.

....

Step 4: Review.

Does the answer match the question?
Yes, the problem asked for a number of doughnuts.

Did the plan work for the problem? **Yes.**

Is there another way you could solve the problem?
Yes, there are many other ways to solve the problem.

If you recognized that the problem was multiplication, you could go directly to using an equation.

You could also have drawn the picture, then count the number of doughnuts.

Another way to solve the problem is to add 6 doughnuts for each package of doughnuts that Matt ate.
(6 + 6 + 6 + 6 + 6 + 6 + 6 = 42)

It does not matter which plan you use, the answer is always 42 doughnuts.

⑥ Basic Facts

A large one-topping pizza that usually costs $12 is only $9 when you buy three or more. The National Honor Society is ordering pizza for students who help decorate for homecoming. How much will 8 one-topping pizzas cost?

Step 1: Understand the problem.

Read the problem. Is there anything you do not understand?

What does the problem ask you to find?
The cost for 8 one-topping pizzas.

What information do you need to solve the problem?
You need to know the cost of each one-topping pizza.

Is all of the information you need in the question? Is there extra information?
This problem gives you information on the regular price of a one-topping pizza, and the price when you buy three or more of them. Since you are finding the price for 8 pizzas, the regular price of the pizza is extra information.

Step 2: Make a plan.

Let's write an equation to solve this problem.

Step 3: Follow the plan.

The problem asks the cost for 8 pizzas that each cost $9. Write the equation in words first, then change the words to numbers and math symbols.

<u>number of pizzas</u> <u>times</u> <u>price per pizza</u> <u>is</u> <u>total cost</u>

8 × \$9 = \$72

The cost for 8 one-topping pizzas is \$72.

....

Step 4: Review.

Does the answer match the question?
Yes. The problem asked for a cost.

Does the answer make sense? **Yes.**

Did the plan work for the problem? **Yes.**

Know your facts!

Memorizing the basic multiplication facts makes solving problems that have larger numbers much easier.

⑦ Powers of Ten

A cell phone plan lets you buy minutes in groups of 100 or 1,000. When you buy 100 minutes, each minute costs 5.5¢. When you buy 1,000 minutes, each minute costs you 3¢. What is the total cost for 1,000 minutes?

Step 1: Understand the problem.

Read the problem. Is there anything you do not understand?

What does the problem ask you to find?
The cost of 1,000 minutes of cell phone time.

What information do you need to solve the problem?
Is there extra information?
You need to know the cost for one minute when you buy 1,000 minutes. There is extra information. You do not need to know the cost per minute when you buy 100 minutes.

Step 2: Make a plan.

This problem tells you the cost of one minute, and asks for the cost of many. It is a multiplication problem. One of the factors is a power of ten, so let's use mental math.

Step 3: Follow the plan.

The problem asks for the total cost of 1,000 minutes when each minute costs 3¢. Multiply 1,000 × 3 using mental math.

To multiply any number by a power of ten, count the zeros in the power of ten, and put the same number of zeros on the right end of the other factor.

There are three zeros in 1,000. Put three zeros on the right end of the other factor, 3.

Think: 1,000 × 3¢ = 3,000

The answer is 3,000, so the total cost is 3,000¢. Money values over 99¢ are normally written as dollars instead of cents. Since 100¢ equals $1.00, 3,000¢ is the same as $30.00.

The total cost for 1,000 minutes of cell phone time is $30.00.

Step 4: Review.

Does the answer match the question?
Yes. The problem asks for a cost.

Did the plan work for the problem? **Yes.**

Is there another way you can solve the problem?
Yes. You can multiply the factors on paper.

```
   1,000
 ×      3
 ───────
   3,000
```

8 Multiples of Ten

There are 8 members in Jenna's science club. Each member planted 30 pine trees as a community service project. How many trees did the club members plant in all?

Step 1: Understand the problem.

Read the problem. Is there anything you do not understand?

What does the problem ask you to find?
The number of trees planted by the club members.

What information do you need to solve the problem?
The number of members in the club, and the number of trees each member planted.

Step 2: Make a plan.

Because each member planted the same number of trees, this is a multiplication problem. Let's use mental math and basic facts.

Multiples of Ten and Basic Facts

Factors that include multiples of ten can be multiplied using basic multiplication facts.

1. Ignore the zeros.	30 X 8
2. Multiply the basic fact.	3 X 8 = 24
3. Put the number of zeros that you ignored on the right end of the product.	30 X 8 = 240

Step 3: Follow the plan.

Each of the 8 members planted 30 pine trees. You can use mental math to find the product of 8 × 30 using the basic multiplication fact 8 × 3 = 24.

Think: Since 8 × 3 = 24, 8 × 30 = 240

The members of Jenna's science club planted 240 pine trees in all.

Step 4: Review.

Does the answer match the question?
Yes. The problem asked for the total number of trees.

Did the plan work for the problem? **Yes.**

Is there another plan you can use to solve the problem? **Yes. You can draw a picture, or do the multiplication on paper.**

A saxophone reed costs $3 when the reeds are sold in a case of 4 reeds. The band has 25 saxophone players. What would be the total cost if every player buys a case of reeds?

Step 1: Understand the problem.

Read the problem. Is there anything you do not understand? What does the problem ask you to find? **The cost if every player purchased a case of reeds.**

What information do you need to solve the problem? **How many saxophone players there are and the cost of a case of reeds.**

Step 2: Make a plan.

This problem has more than one step. It can be solved by writing an equation with more than one operation.

Step 3: Follow the plan.

You can find the cost of a case of reeds by multiplying the cost of one reed by the number of reeds in the case.

cost of one reed $\times$ **number in case = cost of one case**

To find the cost of a case of reeds for each player, multiply the cost of one case of reeds by the number of players.

cost of one case $\times$ **number of players = total cost**

To find the total cost in one equation, multiply the cost of one reed by the number of reeds in a case, then multiply again by the number of players.

cost of one reed $\times$ **number in case** $\times$ **number of players = total cost**

Multiplication Properties

The Associative Property: Changing the grouping of the factors does not change the product.

$$(4 \times 2) \times 3 = 4 \times (2 \times 3)$$

The Commutative Property: Changing the order of the factors does not change the product.

$$8 \times 7 = 7 \times 8$$

The Identity Property: The product of one and any number is the other number.

$$1 \times 32 = 32 \text{ and } 97 \times 1 = 97$$

The Inverse Property: The product of inverses is 1.

$$(3/2) \times (2/3) = 1$$

The Zero Property: The product of a number and zero is zero.

$$62 \times 0 = 0$$

Replace the words with numbers. Then multiply.

$3 × 4 × 25 = total cost

The associative property says it doesn't matter which two factors you multiply first. When you multiply the 4 and 25 first, the problem can be solved using mental math.

Think: 4 × 25 = 100. Then 3 × 100 = 300.

It will cost $300 for every player to buy a case of reeds.

Step 4: Review.

Does the answer match the question?
Yes. The problem asked for a total cost.

Did the plan work for the problem? **Yes.**

Check the answer using multiplication without the associative property. Is the answer the same? **Yes.**

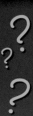

Students earn $7 toward their sports fees each time they clean the stands after a game. Taylor cleaned after 13 games this season. How much did he earn in total?

Step 1: Understand the problem.

Read the problem. Is there anything you do not understand? What does the problem ask you to find?
The total amount of money that Taylor earned cleaning the stands.

What information do you need to solve the problem?
The amount he earned each time he cleaned and how many times he cleaned.

Is there any extra information? **No.**

Step 2: Make a plan.

This is a multiplication problem. Let's break the problem into parts using the distributive property.

The Distributive Property

The distributive property states that if one of the factors in a multiplication problem is a sum, it can be solved two ways.

1. Add first then multiply.
    (2)(3 + 3) = (2)(6) = 12
2. Multiply each addend (distribute), then add.
    (2)(3 + 3) = (2)(3) + (2)(3) = 6 + 6 = 12

Step 3: Follow the plan.

Taylor earned $7 for each of the 13 times he cleaned.

<u>dollars per cleaning</u> <u>times</u> <u>number of times cleaned</u> = <u>total</u>

$7 × 13 = Total

The distributive property lets you split one of the factors into an addition expression. Let's split the factor 13 into 10 + 3 to make the multiplication easier.

$7 × (10 + 3) = Total
($7 × 10) + ($7 × 3) = Total
  ($70)   +   ($21)   = $91

Taylor earned $91 toward his sports fees.

Step 4: Review.

Does the answer match the question?
Yes. The problem asked for a total dollar amount.

Did the plan work for the problem? **Yes.**

Is there another way to solve the problem? **Yes. You could use a model to count out 13 sets of $7 each. Or you could do the multiplication without using the distributive property.**

Brad drove 56 miles in one hour. About how many miles can he drive in 9 hours?

Step 1: Understand the problem.

Read the problem. Is there anything you do not understand?

What does the problem ask you to find?
About how many miles Brad can drive in 9 hours.

Do you have all of the information you need to solve the problem?
Yes, you know how far Brad drove in one hour.

Step 2: Make a plan.

Estimation problems ask you to find an answer that is close to the exact answer. Problems that use words such as *about, approximately, around, estimate, guess, nearly,* and *roughly* may tell you the problem uses estimation.

This problem tells you the distance Brad drove in one hour, and asks you to find an approximate distance for more than one hour. This is a estimation problem that uses multiplication.
Let's estimate using rounding.

Step 3: Follow the plan.

If Brad drove 56 miles each hour for 9 hours, you could multiply 56×9 to find the exact number of miles he traveled. To estimate the distance he can travel, you can round the number of miles to the nearest ten, then multiply.

56 rounds up to 60

$60 \times 9 = 540$

Brad can drive about 540 miles in 9 hours.

Step 4: Review.

Does the answer match the question?
Yes. The problem asked for an estimated number of miles.

Find the exact answer, and compare it to the estimate.
$56 \times 9 = 504$. The estimated answer is close to the exact answer.

Could you have used other numbers to estimate the answer? **Yes. You could have also rounded the 9 to 10.
$60 \times 10 = 600$.**

Why is the estimate of 540 miles better than the estimate of 600 miles? **The estimate of 600 miles is not as close to the exact answer, 504 miles. In this problem, if you round 56 up to 60, the estimated answer will be greater than the exact answer. If you also round 9 up to 10, you are rounding both of the original numbers up. This makes the estimated answer even greater.**

⑫ Multiplying Larger Numbers

In Courtney's school district, the school year is 184 school days. Courtney has 5 full school years left before she graduates. How many school days are there before Courtney graduates?

Step 1: Understand the problem.

Read the problem. Is there anything you do not understand?

What does the problem ask you to find?
The number of school days until Courtney graduates.

What information do you need to solve the problem?
The number of years until Courtney graduates, and the number of school days in each year.

Step 2: Make a plan.

You are given the number of days in one school year, and asked to find the number of days in 5 school years. This is a multiplication problem. Write a multiplication equation.

Step 3: Follow the plan.

Write the equation in words first.

Days per school year times number of school years left = school days before graduation

Replace the words with numbers. Then multiply.

184×5 = school days before graduation

Since 184 is a large number (more than one digit) use a paper and pencil to multiply.

$$\begin{array}{r} 42 \\ \mathbf{184} \\ \times \mathbf{5} \\ \hline \mathbf{920} \end{array}$$

Courtney has 920 school days before she graduates.

Step 4: Review.

Does the answer match the question?
Yes. The problem asked for a number of days.

Is the answer reasonable?
Use estimation to check your answer. Round the number of school days to the nearest hundred. 184 rounds up to 200. Multiply 200 × 5 = 1,000. Since you rounded up, the estimated answer should be slightly higher than the correct answer. 1,000 is slightly higher than 920. The answer is reasonable.

⑬ Partial Products

Tickets for a concert are $12 per person. If 218 people buy tickets, what is the total amount in ticket purchases?

Step 1: Understand the problem.

Read the problem.

What does the problem ask you to find?
The total amount in ticket purchases.

Do you have all of the information you need to solve the problem?
Yes. You know the price for one ticket and the number of tickets purchased.

Always read a problem more than once while you are solving it. Make sure you are looking for what the question is asking for.

Step 2: Make a plan.

You know the price of one ticket, and need to find the price for more than one ticket. This is a multiplication problem.
The numbers in this problem both have more than one digit. Let's multiply using partial products.

....

Step 3: Follow the plan.

Multiply the number of people who buy tickets by the price of each ticket to find the total amount in ticket purchases.

218 × 12 = total

Multiply the first factor, 218, by the ones digit of the second factor, 2. This answer is called a partial product because it is part of the total product.

$$\begin{array}{r} 218 \\ \times\ \ 2 \\ \hline 436 \end{array}$$

Multiply the first factor, 218, by the tens digit of the second factor, 10.

$$\begin{array}{r} 218 \\ \times\ \ 10 \\ \hline 2{,}180 \end{array}$$

Add the partial products.

$$\begin{array}{r} 2{,}180 \\ +\ \ 436 \\ \hline 2{,}616 \end{array}$$

The total amount in ticket purchases was $2,616.

....

Step 4: Review.

Does your answer match the question?
Yes, the problem asked for a total dollar amount.

Is the answer reasonable?
Yes. If you round both factors to the greatest place value, you can use mental math to multiply 200 x 10 = 2,000. More than 200 people purchased tickets, and each ticket price was more than $10, so the answer will be greater than $2,000.

Why can you add partial products in multiplication?
The distributive property lets you split one of the factors. (See pages 24 and 25.)

Multiplying Decimals

A flavored iced coffee costs $3.19, including tax. Hannah had vanilla, Charlene had chocolate mint, and Kiona had hazelnut. How much did the girls pay for their coffee in all?

Step 1: Understand the problem.

Read the problem. Is there anything you do not understand?

What does the problem ask you to find?
The total amount the girls paid for their coffee.

What information do you need to solve the problem? **The price of each coffee, and the number of coffees that were purchased.**

Is all of the information that you need in the question? **Yes. You need to count the number of girls in the problem to find the number of coffees that were purchased.**

Step 2: Make a plan.

Count the number of girls who purchased a coffee. You can use multiplication because each coffee was the same price. Write a multiplication equation.

Step 3: Follow the plan.

Hannah, Charlene, and Kiona each bought a coffee, so 3 coffees were purchased.

Write the equation in words first.

price per coffee times number of coffees = total amount

To multipy decimals, ignore the decimal point. Multiply just as with whole numbers.

Count the places on the right of the decimal point in the factors.

Put a decimal point in the answer so that there are the same number of places on the right.

Replace the words with numbers. Then multiply.

$3.19 × 3 = total amount

$$
\begin{array}{r}
\overset{2}{} \\
\$3.19 \\
\times \quad 3 \\
\hline
\$9.57
\end{array}
$$

The girls paid $9.57 in all for their coffee.

Step 4: Review.

Does the answer match the question? **Yes. The problem asked for a total dollar amount.**

Check the answer. **Sometimes you can check your answer using a calculator. If the problem is on homework, or a test, make sure you ask for permission first. Or, you can add.**

$$
\begin{array}{r}
\$3.19 \\
\$3.19 \\
+\ \$3.19 \\
\hline
\$9.57
\end{array}
$$

Lawrence works in a flower shop. He takes an order for 24 roses. The customer wants 1/2 of the roses to be red, 1/3 of the roses to be yellow, and the rest to be pink. How many pink roses does he need for the order?

Step 1: Understand the problem.

Read the problem. Is there anything you do not understand?

What does the problem ask you to find?
The number of pink roses Lawrence needs for the order.

What information do you need to solve the problem?
The total number of roses, the fraction of roses that are red, and the fraction of roses that are yellow.

Is there extra information? **No, there is no extra information.**

Step 2: Make a plan.

One way to solve this problem is to find the number of red and yellow roses, then subtract from the total number of roses.

When a fractions problem uses the word "of" after a fraction, it is a multiplication problem. You can find the number of red and yellow roses using multiplication.

Step 3: Follow the plan.

The problem tells you that 1/2 of the total roses are red.

<u>fraction</u> of <u>total roses</u> = <u>number of red roses</u>

Replace the words with numbers and symbols. Do the multiplication.

$$\frac{1}{2} \times \frac{24}{1} = \frac{(1)(24)}{(2)(1)} = \frac{24}{2} = \frac{12}{1} = \text{12 red roses}$$

The problem tells you that 1/3 of the total roses are yellow.

fraction of total roses = number of yellow roses

Replace the words with numbers and symbols. Do the multiplication.

$$\frac{1}{3} \times \frac{24}{1} = \frac{(1)(24)}{(3)(1)} = \frac{24}{3} = \frac{8}{1} = \text{8 yellow roses}$$

Now subtract.

total roses	minus	red roses	minus	yellow roses	=	pink roses
24	-	12	-	8	=	4

Lawrence needs 4 pink roses for the order.

Step 4: Review.

Does the answer match the question?
Yes. The problem asks for the number of pink roses.

Check your answer. **Add the total for each color of roses.**

```
  12 red roses
   8 yellow roses
+ 4 pink roses
─────────────────
  24 roses in all
```

Autumn helps coach a summer soccer program for elementary students. There are 32 students who are divided evenly into 4 teams. How many students are on each team?

Step 1: Understand the problem.

Read the problem. Is there anything you do not understand?

What does the problem ask you to find?
The number of students on each team.

What information do you need to solve the problem?
The total number of students and the number of teams.

Is all of the information that you need in the question? **Yes.**

Step 2: Make a plan.

This problem tells you that there are 32 students divided evenly into 4 teams. Problems that give you a total for many and ask you to find a value for one are often division problems. Problems that use words such as *average, divided, evenly, equally, per, shared,* and *split* may be division problems.

Let's write a division equation.

Division starts with an amount and separates it into groups of equal sizes.

You can use division to find the number of groups, or the size of each group.

Step 3: Follow the plan.

Write the equation in words first.

total students **divided by** **number of teams** = **students per team**

32 ÷ 4 = 8 students per team
There are 8 students on each team.

....

Step 4: Review.

Does the answer match the question?
Yes. The problem asked for the number of students on each team.

Is there another way you could have answered the problem?
You could model the problem with 32 items, and divide the items into 4 equal groups, then count the number in a group.

Check your answer.
You can check division answers with multiplication. Multiply your answer by the number you divided by.

8 × 4 = 32

On a field trip to the natural history museum, students must stay in groups of 3. If there are 21 students in all, how many groups are there?

Step 1: Understand the problem.

Read the problem. Is there anything you do not understand?

What does the problem ask you to find?
The number of groups of students on the field trip.

What information do you need to solve the problem? **The total number of students and the number of students in each group.**

Is there any extra information? **No, there is no extra information.**

Inverse Operations and Fact Families

Multiplication and division are **inverse operations**. For each multiplication fact, there is a related division fact that does the opposite. When you know 4 × 2 = 8, then you also know 8 ÷ 2 = 4.

The commutative property tells you that if you know 4 × 2 = 8, you also know 2 × 4 = 8. The related division fact for 2 × 4 = 8 is 8 ÷ 4 = 2.

The four related facts are called a **fact family**.

4 × 2 = 8	8 ÷ 2 = 4
2 × 4 = 8	8 ÷ 4 = 2

Step 2: Make a plan.

The problem tells you the total number of students and that the students are in equal groups. This is a division problem. Let's say you do not remember the division facts, but you do remember the multiplication facts. You can use the inverse operation, multiplication, to solve this problem.

Step 3: Follow the plan.

Write the problem in words.

total students divided into students per group = number of groups

Rewrite the problem as a multiplication problem.

number of groups times students per group = total students

Replace the words with numbers and symbols.

number of groups × 3 = 21

What number times 3 equals 21? **7**

There are 7 groups of students.

Step 4: Review.

Does the answer match the question? **Yes. The problem asked for the number of groups.**

A 4-H club is spending a weekend camping and canoeing. The trip cost is $78, and it is divided into two equal payments. How much is each payment?

Step 1: Understand the problem.

Read the problem. Is there anything you do not understand?

What does the problem ask you to find?
The amount of money for each payment.

Do you have all of the information you need to solve the problem?
Yes, you know the total cost and the number of payments.

Step 2: Make a plan.

The problem tells you the total cost and that the cost is divided into two equal groups. This is a division problem. The numbers in the problem are not a basic division fact. Let's use long division.

Step 3: Follow the plan.

Write the problem in words.

<u>total cost</u> <u>divided by</u> <u>number of payments</u> = <u>cost per payment</u>

Replace the words with numbers and symbols.

$78 ÷ 2 = cost per payment

Write the division problem using the long division symbol.

$2 \overline{)78}$

Divide one place value at a time, beginning on the left.

$$
\begin{array}{r}
39 \\
2\overline{)78} \\
-6 \\
\hline
18 \\
-18 \\
\hline
0
\end{array}
$$

Each payment is $39.

Step 4: Review.

Does the answer match the question?
Yes. The problem asked for the payment, or amount.

Check the answer.
This problem has only two payments. Add the two payments and see if the total is correct.

$39 + $39 = $78

Douglas has 12 weeks of summer break. He can earn a prize package in the summer reading program if he reads at least 30 books. How many books does Douglas need to read each week?

Step 1: Understand the problem.

Read the problem. Is there anything you do not understand?

What does the problem ask you to find?
The number of books Douglas needs to read each week.

What information do you need to solve the problem?
The total number of books he needs to read and the number of weeks he has to read them in.

Step 2: Make a plan.

A total number of books is being divided into a number of weeks.

Let's write a division equation.

Step 3: Follow the plan.

Write the problem in words first.

total books **divided by** **number of weeks** = **books per week**

Replace the words with numbers and symbols.

30 ÷ 12 = books per week

30 does not divide evenly by 12. Write this as a long division problem to find the answer.

$$2\frac{6}{12}$$
$$12\overline{)\ 30}$$
$$\underline{-24}$$
$$6$$

There is a remainder of 6 after all of the places are divided. Write the remainder as a fraction.
The remainder, 6, becomes the numerator.
The denominator is the divisor, 12.

Reduce the mixed fraction to lowest form.

$$2\frac{6}{12} = 2\frac{1}{2}$$

Douglas needs to read $2\frac{1}{2}$ books each week.

Step 4: Review.

Does the answer match the question?
Yes. The problem asks for a number of books for each week.

Does the answer make sense?
Yes. If Douglas reads 2 books a week, after 12 weeks he will have read 24 books. This is 6 less than he needs. If he reads 3 books a week, after 12 weeks he will have read 36 books. This is 6 more than he needs. The answer is between 2 and 3 books a week.

43

⑳ Interpreting Remainders

You can rent a catamaran for 2-hour, 4-hour, and 8-hour excursions. The boats can hold up to four people, and there must be at least two people in each boat. If a group of 13 people are renting boats, what is the least number of catamarans they can rent?

Step 1: Understand the problem.

Read the problem. What does the problem ask you to find?
The least number of catamarans the group can rent.

What information do you need to solve the problem?
The total number of people in the group and the number of people that can go in a catamaran.

Is all of the information that you need in the question? **Yes.**

Is there extra information in the question? **Yes. You do not need to know that you can rent the catamarans for three different lengths of time.**

Step 2: Make a plan.

This problem has a group of people who are being divided into boats. Let's draw a picture to understand and solve this problem.

Step 3: Follow the plan.

There are 13 people in all. Since the problem asks for the least number of boats, you want to fill each boat as full as you can. Up to 4 people can go in each boat. Draw sketches of boats with 4 people in each until you reach 13.

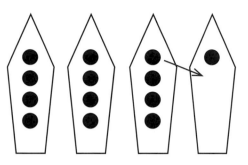

Twelve people fit exactly into 3 boats. There is one person left, so you need at least one more boat. The problem tells you that at least two people must be in each boat. Can this be done? **Yes. Move one person from one of the other boats so that there are two people in the final boat.**

The group must rent at least 4 catamarans.

Step 4: Review.

Does the answer match the question?
Yes. The problem asks for a number of boats.

Could you have done anything differently?
Yes. This is a division problem, so you could write a division equation.

<u>total group</u> <u>divided by people per boat</u> = <u>number of boats</u>

13 ÷ 4 = 3 with a remainder of 1, or $3\frac{1}{4}$ boats

You need to decide what the remainder (the extra person) means. In this problem, you know you can't rent 1/4 of a boat, so you must rent at least one more entire boat, making 4.

There are 9 months in a school year. Using the data shown, how many books were checked out on average per month in the 2008 school year?

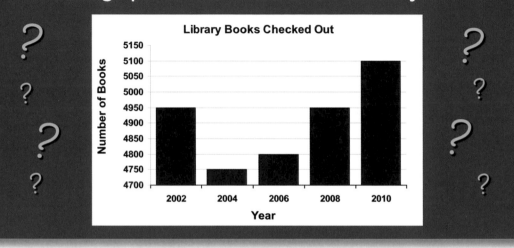

Step 1: Understand the problem.

Read the problem. What does the problem ask you to find?
The average number of books checked out each month of the school year in 2008.

What information do you need to solve the problem?
The total number of books checked out in 2008 and the number of months in the school year.

Is all of the information you need in the problem?
No. The problem does not tell you how many books were checked out in 2008. It does tell you that the information is in the graph that is given.

Step 2: Make a plan.

Find the information you need in the graph. Then divide to find the average number of books.

Step 3: Follow the plan.

Find the year 2008. Look at the bar to see that there were 4,950 books checked out in 2008.

Write the problem in words first.

total books **divided by** **number of months** = **books per month**

Replace the words with numbers and symbols.

4,950 ÷ 9 = books per month

Write this as a long division problem to find the answer.

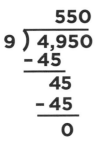

An average of 550 books were checked out each month in 2008.

....

Step 4: Review.

Does the answer match the question?
Yes. The problem asked for an average number of books.

Check the answer.
Multiply the answer, 550, by the number you divided by, 9.

```
   4
  550
×   9
─────
4,950
```

㉒ Find a Pattern

? **Six groups of students distributed 1,800 flyers for a talent show. On average, how many flyers did each group distribute?**

Step 1: Understand the problem.

Read the problem. Is there anything you do not understand?

What does the problem ask you to find?
The average number of flyers that each group distributed.

Is all of the information that you need in the question?
Yes, the problem gives you the total number of flyers and the number of groups that distributed them.

Patterns and Multiples of Ten

When the number being divided is a multiple of ten, you can take off the zeros to use a basic fact, then put the same number of zeros back in the answer.

12 ÷ 3 = 4   120 ÷ 3 = 40   1,200 ÷ 3 = 400

When the number being divided and the number you are dividing by are both multiples of ten, you can take the same number of zeros from each without changing the answer.

27 ÷ 3 = 9   270 ÷ 30 = 9   2,700 ÷ 300 = 9

Step 2: Make a plan.

This problem is looking for an average. It is a division problem. The total number of flyers is a multiple of ten. Let's see if we can use a pattern to solve the problem.

Step 3: Follow the plan.

Write the problem in words first.

total flyers divided by number of groups = flyers per group

Replace the words with numbers and symbols.

1,800 ÷ 6 = flyers per group

Ignore the zeros on the right of 1,800 and use a basic fact.
Put the same number of zeros on the right of the answer that were in the number being divided.

1,800 ÷ 6 = 300

Each group distributed an average of 300 flyers.

Step 4: Review.

Does the answer match the question?
Yes. The problem asked for an average number of flyers.

Check your math.
Multiply.
300 × 6 = 1,800

There are 315 faculty and staff members at the high school. The student council is sending each of them a handmade birthday card. If 21 students volunteer to make the cards, how many must each student make?

Step 1: Understand the problem.

Read the problem. Is there anything you do not understand?

What does the problem ask you to find?
The number of cards each student must make.

What information do you need to solve the problem?
The total number of cards that must be made and the number of students who are making cards.

Step 2: Make a plan.

This problem tells you a number of cards that need to be made and asks you for the number of cards each student must make. This is a division problem. Let's try the guess and check plan.

Step 3: Follow the plan.

Start by making a guess that you think is close to the answer. You can estimate by saying that 315 is close to 300 and 21 is close to 20. 300 ÷ 20 is the same as 30 ÷ 2. 30 ÷ 2 = 15.

Use multiplication to check 15 as the quotient.

```
      21
    × 15
    ─────
     105
   + 210
    ─────
     315
```

The first guess was correct. If the guess had not been correct, you would have had to adjust the answer until it was correct.

Each student must make 15 birthday cards.

Step 4: Review.

Does the answer match the question?
Yes. The problem asks for a number of cards.

Is there another way to solve this problem?
Yes. You could write a division equation and solve it. You could also use a model, or draw a picture.

Is the answer reasonable?
Yes. The guess and check method begins with a reasonable answer. It also checks for accuracy while you are solving the problem.

Dividing a Decimal

Andria and Stefan ate lunch at a cafe and split the bill evenly. The total bill was $16.34. How much did each pay?

Step 1: Understand the problem.

Read the problem. Is there anything you do not understand?

What does the problem ask you to find?
The amount that Andria and Stefan each paid for their lunch.

Do you have all of the information you need to solve the problem?
Yes, you know the total cost of their lunch and that each paid the same amount.

Step 2: Make a plan.

This problem tells you the total bill and asks you to divide it into equal parts. This is a division problem. Let's write an equation.

Step 3: Follow the plan.

Write the problem in words first.

total bill divided by number of people = cost per person

Replace the words with numbers and symbols.

$16.34 ÷ 2 = cost per person

A decimal is being divided by a whole number. Write this as a long division problem. Divide just as a whole number.

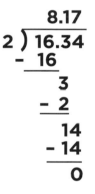

Place the decimal point in the answer above the decimal point in the dividend.

Andria and Stefan each paid $8.17.

Step 4: Review.

Does the answer make sense? **Yes.**

Does the answer match the question?
Yes. The question is how much each paid.

Check the math.
Since there are only two people, you can add the amount that each paid to check for the correct total. $8.17 + $8.17 = $16.34

A box of granola bars has a total weight of 39 ounces. Each granola bar weighs 6.5 ounces. How many bars are there in a box?

Step 1: Understand the problem.

Read the problem. Is there anything you do not understand?

What does the problem ask you to find?
The number of granola bars in a box.

Do you have all of the information you need to solve the problem?
Yes. You know the total weight of the box and the weight of each bar.

Step 2: Make a plan.

You are given the total weight for more than one bar and the weight of one bar. You can divide to find the number of bars. Let's say you do not know how to divide by a decimal. You can use repeated subtraction.

Step 3: Follow the plan.

Begin with the total weight of the box of granola bars. Subtract the weight of one bar at a time until you reach zero. Count the number of bars.

```
    39.0
  -  6.5      one bar
  ─────
    32.5
  -  6.5      two bars
  ─────
    26.0
  -  6.5      three bars
  ─────
    19.5
  -  6.5      four bars
  ─────
    13.0
  -  6.5      five bars
  ─────
     6.5
  -  6.5      six bars
  ─────
       0
```

There are six granola bars in a box.

Step 4: Review.

Does the answer match the question?
Yes. The problem asked for the number of bars in a box.

Is there another way you can solve this problem? **Yes. You can divide 39 by the decimal 6.5. To divide by a decimal, move the decimal point the same number of places in the divisor and dividend.**

39.0 ÷ 6.5 = 390 ÷ 65 = 6

Sara has a 2,700 kilobytes (KB) of data files. She is putting the files into folders that contain 1,000 KB each, or one megabyte (MB). How many megabytes is 2,700 kilobytes?

Step 1: Understand the problem.

Read the problem. What does the problem ask you to find?
The number of megabytes in 2,700 kilobytes.

Do you have all of the information you need to solve the problem?
Yes, you know the number of kilobytes in a megabyte.

Step 2: Make a plan.

This problem can be looked at as converting kilobytes to megabytes, or as a division problem. Sara is dividing the files into folders of 1,000 KB each. Each folder is the same as 1 megabyte. To find the number of megabytes, divide the number of kilobytes by 1,000.

Step 3: Follow the plan.

The number of kilobytes in a folder is 1,000. 1,000 is a power of ten. To divide by a power of ten, you can move the decimal point left. 1,000 has three zeros, so move the decimal point left three places.

2,700 ÷ 1,000 = 2.700

2,700 kilobytes is 2.7 megabytes.

Multiplying and Dividing by Powers of Ten

Powers of ten are numbers that are found by multiplying ten by itself a given number of times.

100 is 10 to the 2nd power because it is 10 x 10.

1,000 is 10 to the 3rd power because 1,000 = 10 x 10 x 10.

To multiply a decimal by a power of ten, move the decimal point right the same number of places as there are zeros.

0.04 × 10 = 0.4   0.04 × 100 = 4   0.04 × 1,000 = 40

To divide a decimal by a power of ten, move the decimal point left the same number of places as there are zeros.

2.0 ÷ 10 = 0.2   2.0 ÷ 100 = 0.02   2.0 ÷ 1,000 = 0.002

Step 4: Review.

Does your answer make sense?

Yes. Since a kilobyte is smaller than a megabyte, there are more kilobytes in a given amount of space than there are megabytes.

57

㉗ Dividing Fractions

? ?
? Mr. Samson's chemistry class has 6 boxes of
? molecular model parts. Today's model uses
? 2/3 of a box. How many models can be made?
? ?

Step 1: Understand the problem.

Read the problem. Is there anything you do not understand?

What does the problem ask you to find?
The number of models that can be made.

Do you have all of the information you need to solve the problem?
Yes. You know how many boxes of parts there are, and how much of a box each model uses.

Step 2: Make a plan.

A diagram can help you understand what is happening. Let's draw a diagram, then decide how to solve the problem.

Reciprocals and Division

Reciprocals are two numbers that have a product of 1.
$1/2$ and $2/1$ are reciprocals because $1/2 \times 2/1 = 1$.
You can find the reciprocal of any fraction by switching the numerator and denominator. The reciprocal of **3/5** is **5/3**.

To divide any number by a fraction, multiply by the reciprocal.
$2/3 \div 4/5$ is the same as $2/3 \times 5/4$.

Step 3: Follow the plan.

Draw a diagram that shows six boxes. The fraction $2/3$ means 2 out of 3 equal parts of a box. Show each of the boxes as three equal parts.

How can you find the number of models that can be made?
Divide the parts into sets that each have 2/3 of a box.

number of boxes divided by number of boxes per model = number of models

Replace the words with numbers and symbols. Then divide.

$6 \div \dfrac{2}{3} =$ **number of models**

$6 \times \dfrac{3}{2} = \dfrac{6}{1} \times \dfrac{3}{2} = \dfrac{9}{1} = 9$ **9 models can be made.**

Step 4: Review.

Does your answer make sense?
Yes. Each model uses less than one box, so there should be more models than boxes.

A total of 437 people have purchased tickets for the school play. The auditorium has seating in rows of 9 seats. If there are 64 rows of seats, are there enough seats for everyone?

Step 1: Understand the problem.

Read the problem. Is there anything you do not understand?

What does the problem ask you to find?
If there are enough seats for all of the people who purchased tickets.

Do you have all of the information you need to solve the problem?
Yes. You know how many people purchased tickets, how many seats are in a row, and how many rows of seats there are.

Step 2: Make a plan.

This problem can be solved using estimation. You do not need to know exactly how many seats are needed unless the number of seats and number of tickets are close to each other. Estimate the number of rows that are needed, and compare it to the number of rows in the auditorium.

Step 3: Follow the plan.

Estimate the number of rows that are needed using division and compatible numbers.

437 seats needed ÷ 9 seats in a row = number of rows needed

Use numbers that are easy to divide to replace the actual numbers. $437 \div 9$

can be changed to

Look at the beginning digits. $450 \div 9$

Decide if they are close to a basic fact. $450 \div 9 = 50$

There need to be around 50 rows of seats.
There are 64 rows of seats.

Yes, there are enough seats for everyone.

Step 4: Review.

Does the answer match the question?
Yes. The problem asked if there will be enough seats.

Is there another way you can solve this problem?
Yes. You can find the exact number of seats by multiplying the number of rows and the number of seats in a row.

$64 \times 9 = 576$

There are 576 seats and 437 people. There are enough seats for everyone.

Further Reading

Books

Abramson, Marcie F. *Painless Math Word Problems.* Hauppauge, N.Y.: Barron's Educational Series, 2001.

Sterling, Mary Jane. *Math Word Problems for Dummies.* Hoboken, N.J.: Wiley Publishing, Inc., 2007.

More math help from Rebecca Wingard-Nelson:

Wingard-Nelson, Rebecca. *Division and Multiplication.* Berkeley Heights, N.J.: Enslow Publishers, Inc., 2008.

Internet Addresses

Banfill, J. *AAA Math.* "Multiplication." © 2009. <http://www.aaamath.com/mul.html>

——. *AAA Math.* "Division." © 2009. <http://www.aaamath.com/div.htm>

The Math Forum. "Ask Dr. Math" © 1994–2009. <http://mathforum.org/library/drmath/sets/ elem_multiplication.html>

<http://mathforum.org/library/drmath/sets/elem_division.html>

Index

A
associative property, 23

B
break apart, 24–25

C
commutative property, 23, 39

D
decimals
    division, 52–57
    multiplication, 32–33
distributive property, 24–25
division
    of decimals, 52–57
    estimation, 60–61
    facts, 48
    of fractions, 58–59
    long division, 40–43
    and multiples of ten, 48–49
    by powers of ten, 56–57
    recognizing, 36–37
    repeated subtraction, 54–55
    symbols, 40
    words, 36
  draw a picture, 14–15

E
estimation
    to check, 31, 43
    division, 60–61

multiplication, 26–27
words, 27
extra information, 16

F
fact families, 39
fractions
    division, 58–59
    multiplication, 34–35

G
graphs, 46–47
guess and check, 50–51

I
identity property, 23
inverse operations, 39
inverse property, 23

M
mental math, 19–21, 56–57
multiples of ten, 20–21, 48–49
multiplication
    count by tens, 12–13
    estimation, 26–27
    facts, 16–17, 20–21
    of fractions, 34–35
    of larger numbers, 28–29
    of multiples of ten, 20–21
    of powers of ten, 18–19
    properties, 22–25
    recognizing, 10–11, 15

Laser Therapy in Glaucoma

Jacob T. Wilensky, M.D.

Associate Professor of Ophthalmology
University of Illinois at Chicago
Director, Glaucoma Service
University of Illinois Eye
and Ear Infirmary
Chicago, Illinois

APPLETON-CENTURY-CROFTS/Norwalk, Connecticut

0-8385-5614-0

Notice: Knowledge in the clinical sciences is constantly changing. As new information becomes available, changes in treatment and in the use of drugs become necessary. The author(s) and the publisher of this volume have taken care to make certain that the doses of drugs and schedules of treatment are correct and compatible with the standards generally accepted at the time of publication. The reader is advised to consult carefully the instruction and information material included in the package insert of each drug or therapeutic agent before administration. This advice is especially important when using new or infrequently used drugs.

85 86 87 88 89 / 10 9 8 7 6 5 4 3 2 1

Prentice-Hall International, Inc., London
Prentice-Hall of Australia, Pty. Ltd., Sydney
Prentice-Hall Canada, Inc.
Prentice-Hall of India Private Limited, New Delhi
Prentice-Hall of Japan, Inc., Tokyo
Prentice-Hall of Southeast Asia (Pte.) Ltd., Sinapore
Whitehall Books Ltd., Wellington, New Zealand
Editora Prentice-Hall do Brasil Ltda., Rio de Janeiro

Library of Congress Cataloging in Publication Data
Main entry under title:

Laser therapy in glaucoma.

    Papers presented at a course held Mar. 1982 at the University of Illinois Eye and Ear Infirmary.   Includes index.
    1. Glaucoma—Surgery—Addresses, essays, lectures.
2. Lasers in surgery—addresses, essays, lectures.
I. Wilensky, Jacob T., 1942–   . (DNLM: 1. Glaucoma—surgery—congresses.   2. Lasers—therapeutic use—congresses. WW 290 L343 1982]
RE871.L34 1985   617.7'41059   84-16774
ISBN 0-8385-5614-0

PRINTED IN THE UNITED STATES OF AMERICA

Contributors

Hugh Beckman, M.D.
Associate Professor of Clinical Ophthalmology
Wayne State University
Detroit, Michigan

C. Davis Belcher III, M.D.
Assistant in Ophthalmology
Harvard Medical School
Cambridge, Massachusetts

Stephen R. Deppermann, M.D.
Assistant in Ophthalmology
Harvard Medical School
Cambridge, Massachusetts

Edward Goldman, M.D.
Resident in Ophthalmology
University of Illinois Eye and Ear Infirmary
Chicago, Illinois

Lee M. Jampol, M.D.
Professor and Chairman
Department of Ophthalmology
Northwestern University Medical School
Chicago, Illinois

Marc F. Lieberman, M.D.
Assistant Clinical Professor of Ophthalmology
University of California, San Francisco
San Francisco, California

Irvin P. Pollack, M.D.
Associate Professor of Ophthalmology
Johns Hopkins University
Baltimore, Maryland

Alan L. Robin, M.D.
Assistant Professor of Ophthalmology
Johns Hopkins University
Baltimore, Maryland

Richard J. Simmons, M.D.
Associate Clinical Professor of Ophthalmology
Harvard Medical School
Cambridge, Massachusetts

Bradford J. Shingleton, M.D.
Clinical Assistant in Ophthalmology
Harvard Medical School
Cambridge, Massachusetts

Omah S. Singh, M.D.
Director of Research
New England Glaucoma Research Foundation, Inc.
Boston, Massachusetts

John V. Thomas, M.D.
Clinical Assistant in Ophthalmology
Harvard Medical School
Cambridge, Massachusetts

Jacob T. Wilensky, M.D.
Associate Professor of Ophthalmology
University of Illinois at Chicago
Director, Glaucoma Service
University of Illinois Eye and Ear Infirmary
Chicago, Illinois

Contents

Preface

In the last several years, the application of laser techniques has revolutionized the therapy of glaucoma. In 1979, laser trabeculoplasty was almost unheard of, and the few people who knew about it were highly skeptical. Today, it has become a widely accepted alternative to surgical therapy of open-angle glaucoma. Similarly, before 1980, laser iridotomy was restricted to only a handful of major medical centers. Today, surgical iridectomies are beginning to be an endangered species. Perhaps lasers have produced the greatest change of all in the area of neovascular glaucoma, where a dreaded entity that almost universally resulted in blindness and frequently in enucleation can now be treated successfully. Thus, the laser has become a central part of routine glaucoma care. The practicing ophthalmologist either must be able to perform these various techniques personally or must be willing to refer these patients to another therapist.

This fast moving advancement into laser technology has presented somewhat of a problem to the ophthalmic community. Lasers were first introduced into ophthalmology around 1970, and it was not until the middle of that decade that they really became widely available in ophthalmology training programs. Thus, the majority of today's practicing ophthalmologists have had no training in the use of a laser during their residency, even for retinal procedures. In order for them to become accomplished laser therapists in the treatment of glaucoma, they first must learn to use the laser before they can acquire specific glaucoma techniques.

In response to this need, a number of courses have been presented around the country that have included both didactic training on the applications of the laser to glaucoma as well as practical sessions that have allowed the participants to gain some familiarity with the use of the laser itself. One such course was held at the University of Illinois Eye and Ear Infirmary in March of 1982, and this volume was based upon that meeting. During the meeting I was struck by the fact that all the speakers very diligently listened as their colleagues spoke, frequently taking quite copious notes. We were surprised to discover how much we varied on many technical points, particularly in the technique of laser iridotomy. I think

each of the speakers learned from one another, and I know from subsequent conversations with them that they have incorporated certain newly learned details into their own techniques. If nothing else, I hope that this volume will give the reader an appreciation of the great variety of techniques that can be successfully employed in performing laser iridotomy. Various combinations of laser spot size, duration, and power of burns can be made to yield very similar results with the color of the iris, the equipment tht the therapist has available, and a personal factor that determines which particular combination should be used on any one occasion. Readers should recognize that what is presented in this book constitutes guidelines and perhaps a starting place, but they must go forward based on their own experience and results to develop their own techniques and not just blindly mimic what some "expert" is recommending.

One note of caution must be made. The field of laser therapy of glaucoma is a very dynamic and rapidly changing one. Some of the information presented in this volume will be outdated even before it is printed. Already I am performing trabeculoplasties and iridotomies somewhat differently today than when I began working on this volume. The reader must keep up with the literature to follow these developments or else the patient will not necessarily be given the best of care. Also, it must be remembered that the laser is a two-edged sword. Its use can be beneficial, but it also can be detrimental. Laser energy directed to the wrong place, in too great an intensity, or to too great an extent can cause serious damage to an eye and even result in blindness. The laser is a potent tool that must be used carefully and judiciously. If the reader does not have practical experience with a laser, just reading this book is not enough preparation to treat patients. Practical experience with animal eyes and working with an experienced therapist are essential before the individual ophthalmologist can start to treat patients.

A book of this nature requires the help and cooperation of many people, and I would like to take this opportunity to thank some of those who are responsible for this volume: First, the contributing authors. Not only did they prepare excellent oral presentations for the meeting, but they very studiously updated their papers into a final and current manuscript for incorporation in this book. In addition, they also carefully reviewed the transcript of their comments during the question and answer sessions to make sure that it accurately and completely represented their thoughts. Next, thanks is given to Maxine Gere who provided invaluable editorial assistance in the preparation of this volume. Windy Boyd and Dorris Brown did yeomanly duties in providing the secretarial support needed. Finally, special appreciation must be given to Sue Korienek of the University of Illinois' Office of Continuing Education Services. Sue served as the program coordinator for the symposium, and without her efforts the meeting never could have taken place.

Jacob T. Wilensky, M.D.

CHAPTER 1

An Introduction to Lasers

Hugh Beckman

Photocoagulation for glaucoma therapy dates back to the work of Meyer-Schwickerath. In 1956, he used a xenon arc photocoagulator to produce iridectomies in aphakic eyes. The first operating laser was developed in 1960 by Maiman. The first commercial laser appeared a year later, and within another year pulsed ruby lasers were being used for ophthalmic applications. Much of the early interest was directed to the retina but the anterior segment was not ignored. Zweng and associates reported difficulty in creating iridectomies in pigmented rabbit eyes using low energy ruby lasers. By 1971, Beckman achieved penetrating iridectomies in rabbits and in glaucomatous human eyes with a specially designed high-powered ruby laser.

Attempts to decrease aqueous inflow were made in 1971 by Lee and Pomerantz with argon lasers to ablate the ciliary process in rabbits. They called this method transpupillary argon laser cyclophotocoagulation. In 1972, Beckman described transscleral ruby laser irradiation of the ciliary body in the treatment of intractable human glaucoma. The next year Beckman reported the first argon laser iridectomies in humans, which were followed by successful protocols by Abraham and Pollack. This work in glaucoma went relatively unnoticed until 1973, when Krasnov reported on the use of a Q-switched ruby laser to perform a technique he called laseropuncture, and Hager described two argon laser protocols to treat open-angle glaucoma. These reports, together with the work of Worthen and Wickham who developed protocols for argon laser trabeculotomy, began to stimulate some interest among the ophthalmic community. This

interest was, however, still sporadic, and Simmons' report on the use of argon laser for goniophotocoagulation went relatively unnoticed. It was not until 1979, when Wise and Witter published their first paper on argon laser trabeculoplasty for control of open-angle glaucoma, that laser therapy for glaucoma really began.

With the simultaneous reporting at the Academy in 1981 by Schwartz and Wilensky and Jampol of their studies corroborating Wise's original report, the laser as a means of treating glaucoma became credible. At the same meeting, Ritch and Quigley reported on argon laser iridotomy, and the laser became an acceptable and standard method of glaucoma treatment.

Laser therapy of glaucoma depends on a certain understanding of basic laser physics and how laser energy interacts with tissue. The word *laser* is an acronym for *l*ight *a*mplification by *s*timulated *e*mission of *r*adiation. A laser is a device that emits photons of light much in the same manner of an ordinary light bulb. This light is produced in a way that creates a more efficient use of the energy produced. The wavelength of the light depends on the lasing medium utilized. The lasing medium can be molecular, such as in the carbon dioxide laser, in which the molecules vibrate to cause the emission of photons. If ions are used, as in argon laser, the ions oscillate to cause the emission of photons. The type of laser that I will use here to explain how a laser works is the atomic laser, such as the ruby or neodymium system. A ruby crystal or rod consists of chromium atoms doped into a substrate. Similarly a neodymium laser has neodymium atoms doped into a substrate, which frequently is composed of yttrium, aluminum, and garnet (YAG).

In nature, atoms exist in either an excited or unexcited state. In the unexcited, or ground state, the electrons orbit close to the nucleus (Fig 1) and have less energy. In the excited state, they orbit further from the nucleus and have more energy. As an atom in the ground state absorbs a photon of a given frequency, the energy absorbed will cause the electron to jump from an inner to an outer ring, placing the atom in an excited state. If this electron now jumps from the outer ring back to the inner ring, a photon of fixed frequency is emitted (Planck's constant), and spontaneous emission occurs. Simply stated, if one takes an electron that is in the ground state and flashes light onto it so that it is stimulated, the electron will then go into the outer ring, and the incident photon will be absorbed. This is what generally happens in nature. If light is shone on a substance and it is absorbed, an electron shift of the substance has been caused. If an electron is already in the outer ring, and it is allowed to jump down to an inner ring, this is called spontaneous emission. We see spontaneous emission every day, and call it fluorescence. If an atom is already in the excited state and a photon of specific wavelength is added, this will cause the electron in the outer ring to jump into a more inner ring and emit a photon of a frequency that is identical to the one by which

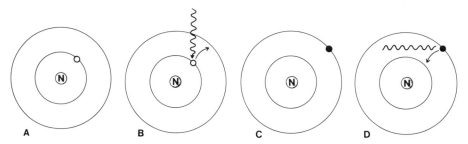

Figure 1. (A) In the ground or unexcited state the electron orbits close to the nucleus. **(B)** When the electron is stimulated by external energy it becomes excited. **(C)** The excited electron jumps to an outer orbit. **(D)** The excited electron spontaneously drops back to the inner orbit, emitting a photon of light energy in the process.

it was stimulated. This process, called stimulated emission, produces out of the system two photons of identical frequency.

With the ruby rod used in solid state ruby laser, a situation is created in which this medium has been preselected to contain a large number of chromium atoms that are in the excited state. A large number of photons are forced in (or pulsed in, as with the argon or carbon dioxide laser), and a large number of atoms that are in the unexcited state are stimulated into an excited state. When the number of atoms in the excited state exceeds the number in the unexcited state, it is called population inversion. As the electrons jump down to their ground state, they emit photons of the same frequency as the ones stimulating them. In the ruby laser, the wavelength of these photons is 6943 angstroms.

These emissions would normally go off in a random fashion in the same manner as light emitted from a light bulb; however they would be no more efficient than a light bulb (Fig. 2). The construction of the laser gives it unique properties. A ruby rod is constructed so that one end is 100 percent reflectile and the other end is 99 percent reflectile (Fig. 3). It is then surrounded with a source of photons, such as those from a flash lamp, and this in turn is surrounded with mirrors, so that all light coming from the flash lamp or from the laser rod is directed back into the cavity to make it more efficient. This whole structure is surrounded by a water jacket, in a water-cooled laser, or by a circulating air cavity, in an air-cooled laser, so that heat given off is carried away and does not destroy the laser components.

The photons of white light are pulsed into the lasing medium. Unexcited atoms are forced into the excited state, and spontaneous emission of 6943 angstrom photons occurs (Fig. 4). These 6943 angstrom photons in turn cause both other unexcited atoms to become excited, and still other excited atoms to fall into the ground state, emitting more photons of 6943

Figure 2. Ordinary white light (**A**) is composed of many different wavelengths that radiate in many different directions. Laser light (**B**) is composed of one wavelength that is traveling in one direction.

angstrom wavelength. This cycle continues with photons bouncing back into the system from the mirrors. Eventually, that portion of the energy that is parallel to the axis of the ruby rod will begin oscillating back and forth at the speed of light between the two mirrored surfaces, until the amount of photons collected exceeds the capacity of the imperfectly re-flectile mirror at one end to retain them within the cavity. At this point, a bolus of energy of a specific wavelength that is highly parallel is emitted coherently by one end of the cavity.

As a result of this process, a propagated beam of light has been designed with certain qualities that are dictated by the method in which it has been created:

1. The light emitted is highly parallel; that is, it has low beam diver-gence, which enables light to be focused into small spot sizes. By focusing it into a small spot size, one can force many photons into a small area. When a large number of photons are focused onto a small area, a high-flux density or high-power density is achieved. If one were to take the finest magnifying glass known and con-verge the rays of the sun at a point, one could achieve 7 W/sq cm. With a typical ruby laser focused to a small spot, one can achieve 1 million W/sq cm.

2. The emitted light is also monochromatic (of one wavelength or frequency). The monochromaticity of the light makes applications

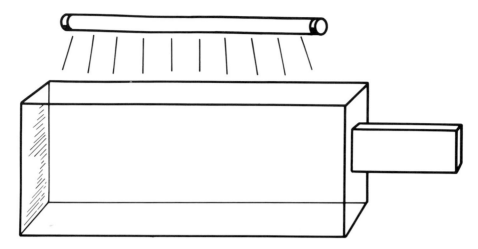

Figure 3. Schematic representation of a laser; the laser consists of a chamber with a totally reflective mirror at one end (*left*) and 99 percent reflective mirror at the other end with an exit channel. The lasing medium is contained within the chamber and is stimulated by the flash tube above. The cooling mechanism is omitted from this diagram.

in ophthalmology predictable, because of the relative transmission and absorption characteristics of one color vis-a-vis another. Thus, argon laser light is transmitted by the optically clear cornea, lens, and vitreous and absorbed by uveal melanin and vascular hemoglobin. Ruby laser light is transmitted by the optically clear media but is less well absorbed by melanin and poorly absorbed by hemoglobin.

3. The emitted light has temporal and spatial coherence. The waves are all in phase with one another (Fig. 5). When the energy arrives, it is in phase with the photons; in this way, they reinforce each other and enable the source of light to have a powerful effect.

When laser energy interacts with biologic tissue, certain linear effects take place. Due to the heat produced, one gets progressive warming, protein denaturation, shrinking, charring and vaporization. In general, tissue burning, charring, shrinking, welding, and poaching are low-power, long-exposure time phenomena. Vaporization, hole formation, and tissue rupture are high-power phenomena. At extremely high-power levels, nonlinear effects, for example, ionization, acoustic shock waves, and plasma formation occur. These effects can be used to disrupt membranes or to tear tissue.

A watt (W) is a unit of power and is defined as 1 joule (J; the unit for measuring energy) of photons being delivered in 1 second. If one were to

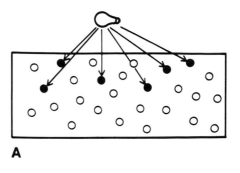

A

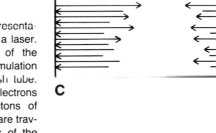

B

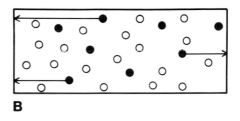

Figure 4. Schematic representation of the functioning of a laser. (**A**) Electrons in some of the atoms are excited by stimulation from the light of the flash tube. (**B**) Some of the excited electrons spontaneously emit photons of light. Those photons that are traveling parallel to the axis of the laser chamber are reflected by the mirrors at the end. (**C**) As more and more photons of light are released, they begin to resonate back and forth across the chamber. (**D**) Finally, the energy level exceeds the capabilities of the 99 percent reflectile mirror and laser emission occurs.

C

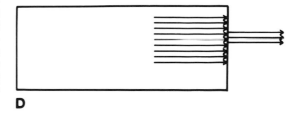

D

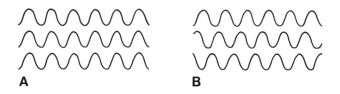

Figure 5. The light waves at (**A**) are of the same frequency and are in phase, i.e., the peaks and valleys of the light waves are identical. The light waves at (**B**) are also of the same frequency but are out of phase.

take a wheelbarrow containing 60 bricks to the top of a building and drop a brick every second for 1 minute, not much damage would be done. You would have dropped 60 bricks, or 1 J worth, and accomplished 1 brick W or 1 brick per second. If one were to take all 60 bricks and drop them all in 1 second, then you would probably damage the sidewalk and would have discharged the same joule of bricks but would have produced 60 brick W of power instead. A watt is the unit of power and a joule is the measurement of energy. The shorter the period of time you discharge the same amount of energy, the higher the power you will produce. Generally, the higher the power produced, the more vaporization takes place. Also, the lower the power and the longer the period of time utilized, the more tissue shrinkage, charring, and poaching occurs.

Given a known amount of energy delivered in a known amount of time, the smaller the spot used to deliver it, the greater the power or energy density. Parameters that might have caused poaching of tissue in a 200-μ spot size may cause vaporization of tissue in a 50-μ spot. Indeed, in a laser such as a Q-switched or mode-locked neodymium:YAG laser, a small number of photons are delivered in a very small spot size in a period of time measured in nanoseconds or picoseconds, yielding millions of watts of power resulting in a nonlinear effect of lasers known as plasma formation or tissue disruption.

Choosing the proper wavelength, power, and spot size enables the ophthalmologist to perform the task appropriately. Examples of this are the large spot size and low-power shrinkage of the pupillary boarder used to enlarge the pupil in argon laser pupilloplasties as opposed to the small spot size, high-power vaporization of the iris performed with the argon laser for iridotomies. What follows in this volume are techniques based on the applications of the knowledge of the transmission and absorption characteristics of the various wavelengths of lasers and the interactions of varying the duration, energy, and size of the laser burns to achieve a therapeutic result.

CHAPTER 2

Laser Trabeculoplasty

Indications

Irvin P. Pollack and Alan L. Robin

INTRODUCTION

*"A glimmer of light is especially bright immediately after the dark."**

The old saying is especially appropriate when one considers how eagerly argon laser trabeculoplasty (ALT) has been welcomed as a new method of treating both primary and secondary open-angle glaucoma. The work of Worthen and Wickham[1,2] established that argon laser energy directed to the trabecular meshwork could reduce the intraocular pressure (IOP). Wise and Witter[3,4] further refined the technique and provided abundant clinical evidence that ALT was not only an important new method for treating open-angle glaucoma, but that its pressure-lowering effect persisted for more than 5 years. Further confirmation of the value of ALT has come from many investigators[5-8] who continue to use the technique suggested by Wise.

We generally use 75 to 100 laser applications that are distributed evenly around the circumference of the anterior chamber angle with a 50-μ spot size for 0.1 second. We use the least amount of power that will produce a visible reaction in the trabecular meshwork, which is usually between 750 and 1200 milliwatts (mW). In our experience, the best results occur when the laser beam traverses the anterior chamber and strikes the midportion of the trabecular meshwork, approximately at the upper

---

*Attributed to Abraham Ben Samuel Hasdai

border of the more pigmented filtering meshwork (Fig. 1). By treating the midportion we avoid the region close to the ciliary body, where stray burns are more likely to cause severe postoperative iritis and high elevations in the IOP in the early postoperative period.

Before discussing the indications for ALT, we wish to interject a brief word about contraindications. These are very few and are based on anatomy rather than on the type of glaucoma. The media must be sufficiently clear to focus the laser on the trabecular meshwork. Thus, corneal edema or severe cornea guttata may preclude treatment. Similarly, if most of the angle is closed by peripheral anterior synechia, then treatment is not possible. As we shall discuss, while ALT may be less effective in certain forms of glaucoma, with the exceptions already noted, there are no definite contraindications to laser treatment.

PRIMARY OPEN-ANGLE GLAUCOMA

Our largest experience has been with the use of ALT in the treatment of primary open-angle glaucoma. In our earliest prospective study of 20 patients with primary open-angle glaucoma, we performed a trabeculoplasty in one eye of each patient and maintained the fellow eye as a control. The IOP for the group fell from a pretreatment mean of 26 mm Hg to a 1 month posttreatment mean of 18 mm Hg, and remained essentially unchanged for a 1-year follow-up period. This represented a 39 percent decrease in IOP, with no significant change in the control eye.

The facility of aqueous outflow in the treated eye increased from a mean of 0.10 to 0.17 in 1 month, and it remained essentially unchanged during he 6 months that tonographic tests were performed. This represented an 80 percent increase in the mean facility of aqueous outflow.

However, the clinical picture was not entirely unblemished. There were originally three additional patients who were not included in the above statistics. Two were patients who were lost to follow-up. The glaucoma of the third patient was entirely uncontrolled by laser therapy, and it required surgical intervention because the IOP remained at levels between 40 and 50 mm Hg after 3 weeks. It is therefore important to realize that even in a homogeneous group of patients such as these, all of whom had primary open-angle glaucoma, certain cases will not respond to laser trabeculoplasty and will require surgery.

Another problem of the laser method is that not all patients respond equally well. In a prospective study of 18 persons with primary open-angle glaucoma, we performed ALT in both eyes and evaluated them for the possibility of maintaining their IOP at a level of less than 22 mm Hg with less medication than was required before treatment. The protocol required that one drug at a time be discontinued until the pressure rose above 21 mm Hg on two successive visits. The drugs were discontinued

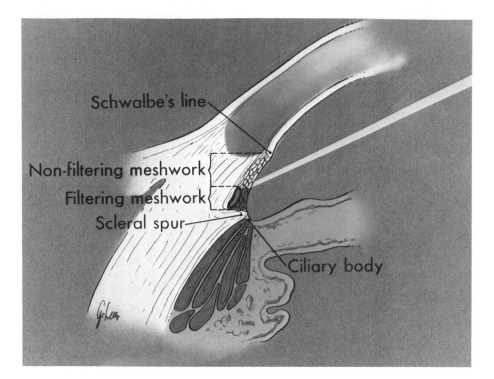

Figure 1. The laser beam was directed through a single-mirror Goldmann gonio-prism so that it came to focus on the uppermost portion of the filtering (pigmented) meshwork. This is approximately midway between the scleral spur and Schwalbe's line. (*From Pollack IP, Robin AL, Ophthalmic Surgery, in press, with permission*).

one at a time in the following sequence: carbonic anhydrase inhibitor, miotic, epinephrine, and timolol. In 5 of the 18 patients (28 percent) who had poorly controlled IOP before treatment, the same medical regimen used preoperatively was required to maintain an IOP of less than 22 mm Hg after laser trabeculoplasty (Fig. 2). Seven patients (39 percent) required less medication, and six cases (33 percent) required no medication after treatment. None of the 18 patients required more than the pretreatment regimen to maintain an IOP of less than 22 mm Hg after trabeculoplasty. Of the nine patients who had required a carbonic anhydrase inhibitor before treatment, six (67 percent) had a controlled IOP without this drug postoperatively. Of the eight patients whose medical regimen before laser treatment included a miotic but no carbonic anhydrase inhibitor, six could discontinue the miotic after ALT. The IOP of one patient receiving timolol therapy was controlled without this drug after trabeculoplasty.

Thus, in this group of patients about one-third could be considered

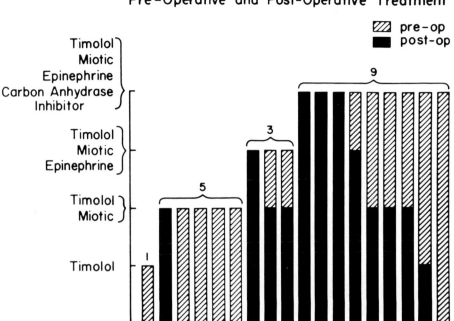

Figure 2. One-third of the eyes required no glaucoma medication after laser trabeculoplasty (*hashed spaces*), and 39 percent required less medication than before. However, 5 of 18 eyes needed all previous medications for IOP control postoperatively (*solid bars*) as was used before trabeculoplasty. (*From Pollack IP, Robin AL, Ophthalmic Surgery, in press, with permission*).

cured, because they require no medical therapy for IOP control; another one-third could be controlled with less medication than before treatment; and one-third required the same medication as before treatment, but their IOP had been brought under control.

The data suggest that the amount of medication required after trabeculoplasty is directly related to the extent of medical therapy required preoperatively. Also, laser trabeculoplasty is excellent for some young persons who need, but cannot tolerate, miotics, and for patients of any age who cannot tolerate carbonic anhydrase inhibitors. Laser trabeculoplasty is the treatment of choice for those persons whose IOP cannot be brought under medical control and for whom surgery is the only alternative. The results also suggest that those persons who are receiving maximal therapy will obtain only limited benefit from ALT. Indeed, this group of patients will probably prove to be the one most likely to not maintain IOP control and to require surgery. Even so, ALT will have "bought" a few years of improved IOP control for such a patient.

SECONDARY OPEN-ANGLE GLAUCOMA

We have found that trabeculoplasty is also a useful treatment for some cases of secondary open-angle glaucoma. Between September 1979 and August 1981, we treated 56 eyes of 47 patients who had this form of glaucoma. These included a wide variety of diagnoses (Table 1) and they were treated in the conventional manner. Whenever feasible, 25 laser applications were made in each quadrant for treatment of the entire trabecular circumference. (When peripheral anterior synechiae precluded effective treatment in a given area, a total of less than 100 burns were applied.)

The results showed that after a mean follow-up of 8 (± 4) months, the IOP in the total group of 56 eyes declined from a mean of 34 mm Hg before treatment to a mean of 22 mm Hg after treatment. Of these 56 eyes, 73 percent had IOP control after treatment, but nearly all eyes (96 percent) required some medication. We considered the treatment a success if it brought the IOP to a level of less than 22 mm Hg. Forty-one eyes (73 percent) met this criterion, but almost half (19 eyes, 46 percent) required the same medication after laser treatment as before. An additional 21 eyes were controlled with less medication.

It appeared that our results were better for certain forms of secondary open-angle glaucoma than for others. Patients with pigmentary dispersion syndrome with glaucoma and exfoliation syndrome with glaucoma responded well to ALT, and in each group the IOP reduction was highly significant. One patient (two eyes) with pigmentary dispersion syndrome required surgery. Because these patients had a well-pigmented trabecular meshwork, the prominent angle landmarks made treatment easier. However, it is important to vary the power according to the response seen in the meshwork, and this response will vary with the amount of pigment present.

TABLE 1. DIAGNOSES OF 300 TREATED EYES

Diagnosis	No. of Eyes
Primary open-angle glaucoma	237
Pseudoexfoliation glaucoma	34
Pigmentary glaucoma	6
Angle recession glaucoma	4
Glaucoma secondary to uveitis	4
Juvenile open-angle glaucoma	3
Congenital glaucoma	3
Iridocorneal endothelial syndrome	3
Steroid-induced glaucoma	2
Glaucoma following congenital cataract extraction	2
Iridocorneal mesodermal dysgenesis	1
Status postprimary angle-closure glaucoma	1

A third group that responded well to ALT was composed of patients who had undergone a prior iridotomy for angle-closure glaucoma or who had open-angle combined with angle-closure glaucoma. In this group the IOP decreased from a preoperative mean of 33 mm Hg to a postoperative mean of 16 mm Hg. Some of these eyes had been treated with a laser iridotomy because of angle-closure, but they either had an elevated IOP soon after this treatment or in later years. An occasional patient was treated for combined-mechanism glaucoma by making a laser iridotomy to open the angle. This was followed by conventional ALT during the same visit or a later one, depending on the amount of pigment dispersion.

To our surprise, patients with surgical aphakia nearly always responded well. (*Editor's Note:* Other observers have not obtained as good results in aphakic patients as Drs. Pollack and Robin are reporting here.) This included not only patients with preexisting open-angle glaucoma who had undergone a cataract extraction, but also those who had undergone a filtering operation before cataract extraction. In both situations, conventional glaucoma surgery is difficult and the results are less than satisfactory. However, after ALT, a fairly pronounced and significant decrease in IOP occurred in nearly all cases. However, this was a somewhat select group of patients, in that they all had few or no peripheral anterior synechia and their glaucoma had been present before as well as after the cataract extraction. In patients with simple aphakia, the IOP declined from a mean of 34 to 17 mm Hg. In those who had both aphakia and a previous filtering procedure, the mean IOP was lowered from 28 to 15 mm Hg.

We had only two patients with Sturge-Weber syndrome, both of whom did well after ALT. The mean IOP decreased from 31 to 17 mm Hg after treatment. This was a dramatic response, and was especially gratifying because surgery for this form of glaucoma is fraught with complications. Filtering procedures are often complicated by intraocular hemorrhage and choroidal effusion and may lead to loss of vision and phthisis.

We observed a less favorable response to ALT in patients with angle-recession glaucoma, uveitic glaucoma, and childhood glaucoma. Nearly 70 percent of these cases required surgery, whereas only 6 percent had IOP control with decreased medication. In many cases a significant reduction in IOP occurred, but the pressure was still very much out of control and surgery was required.

These results suggest that some forms of secondary open-angle glaucoma respond well to ALT. However, poorer results occurred after ALT treatment for childhood, uveitic, and angle-recession glaucoma. Also, 96 percent of the patients still required medication after ALT. Even so, 73 percent were brought under IOP control after this treatment, and many of these could be controlled on less medication.

The good results observed after treatment of some forms of secondary open-angle glaucoma and (in most cases) with primary open-angle glaucoma are certainly encouraging. Although the long-term results of this method are unknown, ALT is a new and exciting form of treatment for suitable cases of glaucoma.

REFERENCES

1. Worthen DM, Wickham MG: Laser trabeculotomy in monkeys. Invest Ophthalmol Vis Sci 12:707, 1973
2. Worthen DM, Wickham MG: Argon laser trabeculotomy. Trans Am Acad Ophthalmol Otolaryngol 78:371, 1974
3. Wise JB, Witter SL: Argon laser therapy for open-angle glaucoma: A pilot study. Arch Ophthalmol 97:319, 1979
4. Wise JB: Long-term control of adult open-angle glaucoma by argon laser treatment. Ophthalmology 88:197, 1981
5. Schwartz AL, Whitten ME, Bleiman B, Martin D: Argon laser trabecular surgery in uncontrolled phakic open-angle glaucoma. Ophthalmology 88:203, 1981
6. Wilensky JT, Jampol LM: Laser therapy for open-angle glaucoma. Ophthalmology 88:213, 1981
7. Pollack IP, Robin AL: Argon laser trabeculoplasty: Its effect on medical control of open-angle glaucoma. Ophthalmic Surg 13:637, 1982
8. Robin AL, Pollack IP: Argon laser trabeculoplasty in secondary forms of open-angle glaucoma. Arch Ophthalmol 101:382, 1983

Technique

Jacob T. Wilensky

Argon laser trabeculoplasty is a deceptively easy procedure to perform; that is, when you watch someone else do it. But when one spends a great many hours teaching this technique to a large number of students, whether residents or practitioners, one finds that it is not nearly as easy a procedure as it appears to be. The experienced therapist actually performs many fine tricks and minute items of technique automatically without thinking. For the novice, these seemingly insignificant points may become major road blocks to obtaining a good result in the patient. Accordingly, an attempt to detail the technique of trabeculoplasty will be made here as thoroughly as possible, so that none of these points will be omitted.

FOCUSING THE LASER

When planning to perform any laser surgery, one must first adjust the laser. The laser has to be as finely focused as possible. To do this, a target is placed in the focal plane of the slit lamp of the laser. A 50-μ sized laser spot is selected, and the slit lamp is focused back and forth until the laser spot is made as small and as sharp as possible. When this is achieved, the slit lamp is locked in place. The two oculars of the slit lamp are then individually focused until each is as sharply focused as is the laser beam. When this has been done, the laser beam and the slit lamp will be exactly parfocal, and the most efficient use of the laser energy will be possible. If the use of a laser is shared, this exercise probably will have to be repeated every time you treat a patient. If there is sole ownership of the laser, then focusing is needed once a week or so to ensure that someone has not accidently moved the oculars, for example, while cleaning the instrument.

ANESTHESIA

Topical anesthesia, such as a single drop of proparacaine hydrochloride (Ophthaine, Ophthetic, Alcaine), is quite sufficient for this procedure. Subconjunctival lidocaine (Xylocaine) or retrobulbar injections are not usually administered but may be necessary (rarely) in patients who constantly move their eyes. During treatment, the patient may complain of an occasional twinge or pinprick, but this is infrequent and is not of sufficient magnitude to interfere with the treatment itself.

GONIOSCOPY LENS

A wide variety of gonioscopic lenses can be used for trabeculoplasty. It is better to choose a lens that uses a methylcellulose bridge between the cornea and the lens because it provides more stability and greater ease in manipulating the eye than do the lenses that use saline or tears. My personal preference is the one-mirror Goldmann lens because of its narrow base and light weight (Fig. 1). Also, the mirror on this lens is relatively closer to the apex of the cornea, and therefore gives a somewhat steeper angle of incidence to the meshwork. This allows one to see into a narrow angle somewhat easier than with the three-mirror Goldmann lens. Many retinal surgeons who have begun to do trabeculoplasties tend to use the three-mirror lens because they are more in the habit of using one, but it does have a wider base, which makes insertion slightly more difficult, and it is heavier than the one-mirror lens. However, no matter which lens is used, the width of the angle can be altered by having the patient move the eyes in the direction of or away from the direction of the mirror.

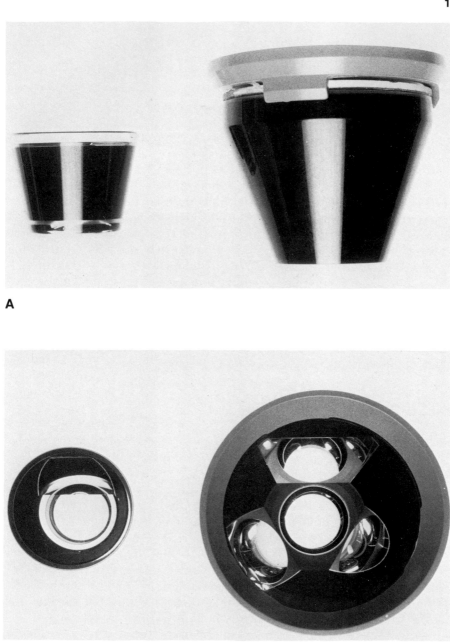

A

B

Figure 1. Comparative sizes of the one-mirror and three-mirror Goldmann goni-oscopy lenses. The one-mirror lens has a smaller base and the mirror inside the lens is closer to the apex of the cornea.

Frequently, the angle that initially appears very narrow can be widened with such manipulation to facilitate the treatment.

ARTIFICIAL WIDENING OF THE ANGLE

Some patients with combined-mechanism glaucoma or previous angle-closure glaucoma may have an extremely narrow angle. In these cases, it may be difficult or even impossible to perform trabeculoplasty without first widening the angle to improve visualization of the trabecular meshwork. There are two techniques that may be used for this purpose. The first is laser gonioplasty, which will be described in greater detail elsewhere in this volume. Briefly, laser gonioplasty involves the use of low-powered, relatively long-duration, and moderately-sized laser burns that are aimed at the peripheral iris roll in such a way as to shrink the iris tissue and flatten it, thereby widening the angle. The second method of widening the angle is to perform a laser iridotomy, which relieves any iris bombé that is present. Again, by using the one-mirror Goldmann gonioscopy lens and having the patient move the eyes, one very rarely has to resort to these procedures to treat satisfactorily patients with narrow angles.

LASER POWER

When Wise and Witter[1] first described laser trabeculoplasty, they recommended that the laser be set at 1000 mW, and then gradually increased in power to as high as 1500 mW until one saw some reaction in the angle such as a faint blanching, pigment dispersion, or a small bubble formation. Many experienced laser therapists in the United States continue to use this technique for determining the laser power; however, they frequently employ a much lower power than the 1000 mW recommended by Wise; in some cases, this may be as low as 400 or 500 mW. A second group uses a standard power for all patients. As a proponent of this second group, this author routinely uses a 900 mW setting on the laser. However, it must be pointed out that there are differences not only among various lasers made by different manufacturers but among different models made by the same manufacturer. Thus, there is probably greater energy attenuation in the mirrored articulated arm of a Coherent 800 laser than there is in a newer model with a fiberoptic delivery system. Also, depending on the state of repair of a laser, it may be emitting more or less energy at different times. Thus, there is always a question whether or not the same power reading on the laser dial translates to an equivalent power at the patient's cornea.

Interestingly, one investigator in St. Louis who had routinely used

a tissue reaction point for selecting his power setting chose a group of patients, determined their reaction point, and treated them with a power setting somewhat below this point. He obtained equally good results with this lower power setting as he did in a comparable series of patients who were treated based on tissue reaction. Thus, it is quite clear that the amount of energy required to create a tissue reaction in many patients is above the amount required to obtain a successful lowering of the intraocular pressure. My own feeling has been that the incidence of postoperative complications such as intraocular pressure rise and inflammation has been reduced since the lower power setting was adopted and for this reason we have chosen to treat the way that we do. We have not altered Wise's original recommendation of using 0.1-second duration burns.

SITE OF BURN PLACEMENT

There has been a great deal of controversy as to where the laser burns should be placed in laser trabeculoplasty. At various times, different investigators have recommended placement anywhere from just above the scleral spur to just below Schwalbe's line. Each has provided various theoretic reasons as to why one particular site is superior to another. Recently, the Boston group has presented a series of patients that compared anterior burns versus posterior burns. They claim that their data indicate that the incidence and magnitude of the postoperative pressure rise were lower in the group that received anterior burns, while the final intraocular pressure lowering effect of the treatment was comparable in both groups. We have noticed that if the laser beam hits the iris root or the ciliary body, it is more painful to the patient and there is a greater likelihood of postoperative inflammation. The more anteriorly one aims, the less likely one is to hit these structures. Therefore, this author has always tended to treat more anteriorly (Fig. 2), and these data from the Boston group only reinforce this tendency.

At this point, a word about gonioscopy in general is appropriate. It is quite obvious that one must be fairly comfortable with the gonioscopic findings and the anatomy of the angle before one can perform laser trabeculoplasty. However, even experienced gonioscopists sometimes have trouble identifying landmarks in certain patients. For this reason, we believe that it is best to begin laser treatment routinely at the 6:00 angle, where the angle is widest and the heaviest amount of pigmentation of the trabecular meshwork is in the inferior angle. These features allow one to identify the anatomic landmarks and be very precise in the localization of the laser burns. As one treats around the angle to the more difficult areas, by staying in the same planes, one can be fairly precise in the burn placement.

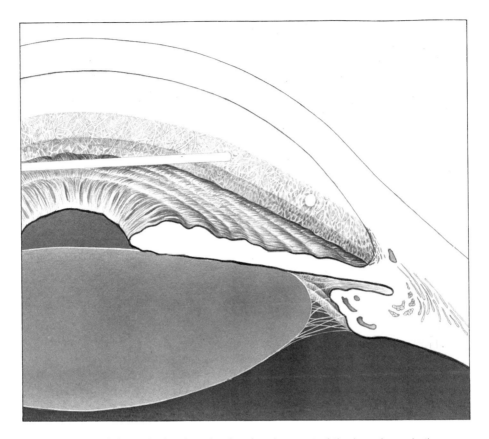

Figure 2. Schematic drawing showing the placement of the laser burns in the anterior trabecular meshwork.

NUMBER OF BURNS

When Wise first devised this technique, on the basis of certain theoretic calculations, he arrived at 100 burns as the ideal number for the treatment. Over the succeeding years, many therapists have begun to vary this by using both fewer and greater numbers of burns. In particular, Thomas and coworkers[2] in Boston divided the therapy into two sessions of 50 burns each in an attempt to reduce the posttreatment rise in intraocular pressure. They found that a significant number of their patients responded very well to just a single 50-burn treatment, and that it was unnecessary to treat the other half of the angle. We have experimented further at the University of Illinois and have treated a small series of patients with only 25 burns over a single quadrant. We found that in many patients this caused a significant lowering of the intraocular

pressure.[3] In most of these patients, however, the treatment of a second quadrant with an additional 25 burns resulted in further lowering the pressure. We currently recommend that a treatment session consist of 50 burns over 180 degrees of trabecular meshwork.

In another study at the University of Illinois, we divided a group of patients and treated half of them with 50 burns over 180 degrees and the other half with 100 burns over 360 degrees. The short-term follow-up of these patients[4] indicated that there was no difference in the amount of pressure lowering achieved. Long-term follow-up of these patients is being conducted, but it is too early to know whether the pressure-lowering effect will persist as long in the group of patients in whom only half of the angle was treated as it does in those whose whole angle was treated. Wise has some retrospective data that suggest that the pressure-lowering effect may be less long-lived in patients receiving fewer treatment spots. It is also interesting that we have a small group of patients in whom only a small or moderate amount of pressure lowering was achieved with 50 burns, who had an additional lowering effect when the other half of the angle was treated. Thus, it appears that there is a continuum of responsiveness in eyes; while some intraocular pressures will drop as much as 10 mm Hg after just 25 laser spots, others require 75 to 100 spots to achieve a similar decrease.

Opinion around the country still varies as to whether the laser treatment should be delivered in divided doses if one is going to treat with more than 50 burns. The views on this seem fairly evenly divided. The study done at the University of Illinois[5] has suggested that there was less immediate posttreatment pressure elevation with 50 burns than with 100 burns. However, some other investigators have obtained different results.

POSTOPERATIVE MANAGEMENT

In general, the biggest complication of laser trabeculoplasty has been the immediate posttreatment intraocular pressure rise that occurs in some patients. We followed up 40 patients at the University of Illinois on an hourly basis for at least 8 hours after trabeculoplasty to allow characterization of the nature of this pressure rise. Based on the results of this study, we believe that if one treats with no more than 50 burns at a session, and if the patient's pressure is monitored hourly for at least 3 hours and no tendency toward elevation of pressure has been detected during this time, then it is safe to allow the patient to go home. If more than 50 burns are applied during a treatment session, the follow-up period must be prolonged because pressure rises 5 or 7 hours after treatment have been documented by several observers. It is particularly important that the

vations, and experiences of all the members of our group practice (Drs. Richard J. Simmons, Thomas M. Richardson, Stephen R. Depperman, C. Davis Belcher, and John V. Thomas).

MECHANISM OF ACTION

Tonographic testing of patients demonstrates a definite increase in the facility of outflow after trabeculoplasty. However, the precise mechanism by which this increase in outflow is mediated is not known.

Wise[6,7] postulated that a possible mechanism for open-angle glaucoma is an age-related stretching of the lamellae of the trabecular meshwork. Since the trabecular meshwork is a ring, this stretching could increase its diameter relative to the more rigid sclera, thereby allowing the lamellae to move outward against each other and against Schlemm's canal. This collapse of lamellae presumably produces a decrease in facility of outflow and an increase in intraocular pressure (IOP).

According to Wise, trabeculoplasty acts by reducing the circumference of the trabecular ring by heat-induced shrinkage of the collagen of the lamellae at numerous points along the inner surface of the ring. Contraction of scar tissue at these burn sites forces the trabecular ring to move toward the center of the anterior chamber, elevating the lamellae and increasing the width of the interlamellar space in areas of untreated meshwork. This action would presumably cause an increase in facility of outflow and a decrease in IOP.

The initial report by Wise and Witter[6] interested us in laser trabeculoplasty, and since 1979 we have been using this procedure to treat patients with medically uncontrolled open-angle glaucoma.

INDICATIONS

At the present time, laser trabeculoplasty is indicated in patients with open angles and uncontrolled IOP on maximally tolerated medical therapy who are candidates for glaucoma surgical intervention. Nearly all the patients we have treated had marked glaucomatous damage to their optic discs with severe visual field loss. Although the technique is less effective in certain types of glaucomas, in aphakic eyes, and in patients under age 40 years, there are as yet no absolute contraindications to its use.

Due to a large number of referrals in New England and elsewhere, we have been fortunate in having had the opportunity to treat a large number of patients with this laser technique in a controlled clinical setting using a rigid protocol.[10] As of January 1982, our group had treated over 600 eyes with laser trabeculoplasty and the indications, techniques, and observations mentioned are based on our continuing experience with

these eyes. The data discussed here deal with the initial 300 eyes of 236 patients treated between December 1, 1979, and July 31, 1981. The average length of follow-up after treatment for these eyes is 5 months.

TECHNIQUE

Patients are treated on an outpatient basis using a continuous wave argon laser. We have obtained equally good results using the Coherent model 900 argon laser and the MIRA model MF 2800 laser. The eye to be treated is anesthetized with one drop of 0.5 percent proparacaine hydrochloride, and a Goldmann three-mirror gonioscopy contact lens with a nonreflective coating is used for treatment to the angle.

The laser settings we employ are similar to those suggested by Wise and Witter.[6] A spot size of 50 μ for a duration of 0.1 second is used. The power is initially set at 1000 mW, and a few test burns are applied. The power is changed, if necessary, to meet three subjective criteria for a desirable burn. When the trabecular meshwork is pigmented, these criteria are a depigmented spot at the point of impact of the laser beam, formation of a few small bubbles, and a minimal scattering of pigment. If the trabecular meshwork is unpigmented, the end point is the formation of a blanched spot on the meshwork. In our patients the power setting ranged from 700 to 1750 mW (average power, 1090 mW).

The laser spots are evenly spaced on the posterior trabecular meshwork immediately anterior to the scleral spur. In pigmented angles, this is the most pigmented portion of the trabecular meshwork. (*Editor's Note:* Dr. Simmons has changed to a more anterior placement of his burns.)

The optimal number of spots that should be applied to the meshwork is not known at the present time. In our patients, we used 100 spots either at one treatment session or divided between two treatment sessions that are separated by a few days to several weeks. If the angle is partially closed with peripheral anterior synechiae, approximately eight spots are applied at each clock hour of open angle.

The first follow-up visit is scheduled 1 to 3 days after treatment. After that, visits are scheduled once a week for 1 month after treatment and then once a month thereafter. It is important that patients be followed closely after treatment, particularly during the first month.

RESULTS

We had the experience of treating several diferent types of glaucoma (Table 1). Success in our patients has been defined as a reduction of IOP that we believe is clinically sufficient to prevent further optic nerve damage and visual field loss and thereby avoid glaucoma surgery. The IOP

TABLE 1. TRABECULOPLASTY IN VARIOUS FORMS OF SECONDARY OPEN-ANGLE GLAUCOMA

Type of Secondary Open-angle Glaucoma	Preoperative IOP[a] (mm Hg)	Postoperative IOP (mm Hg)	Statistical Significance	No. of Eyes Treated (Patients)	No. of Eyes with IOP $\leq$ 22 mm Hg
Pigmentary	32 ± 9	22 ± 8	p < .01	11 (8)	8
pseudoexfoliation	33 ± 8	15 ± 5	p < .05	4 (3)	4
Prior iridotomy for angle-closure	33 ± 10	16 ± 4	p < .05	4 (4)	4
Prior filtering surgery	29 ± 5	18 ± 4	p < .01	7 (6)	6
Aphakic	34 ± 10	17 ± 4	p < .01	6 (4)	6
Aphakic with prior filtering surgery	28 ± 6	15 ± 5	p < .05	5 (5)	5
Congenital	37 ± 5	28 ± 11	p > .2	4 (3)	2
Uveitic	41 ± 5	30 ± 13	p > .1	8 (7)	3
Angle recession	40 ± 12	29 ± 2	p > .1	4 (4)	0
Sturge-Weber syndrome	31 ± 15	17 ± 3	[b]	2 (2)	2

Type of Secondary Open-angle Glaucoma	No. of Eyes Able to Stop at Least One Preoperative Medication	Follow-up (mo)[a]	Age (yr)[a]	Sex (Male:Female)
Pigmentary	7	7 ± 3	38 ± 13	1:7
pseudoexfoliation	3	9 ± 3	70 ± 2	1:2
Prior iridotomy for angle-closure	3	7 ± 2	69 ± 10	2:2
Prior filtering surgery	3	6 ± 1	66 ± 15	3:3
Aphakic	1	7 ± 3	64 ± 18	1:3
Aphakic with prior filtering surgery	2	9 ± 2	61 ± 9	0:5
Congenital	0	12 ± 7	16 ± 3	1:2
Uveitic	1	8 ± 3	54 ± 18	2:5
Angle recession	0	14 ± 2	51 ± 13	2:2
Sturge-Weber syndrome	1	6 ± 0	29 ± 10	1:1

[a]Mean ± one standard deviation.
[b]Not applicable.

TABLE 2. INTRAOCULAR PRESSURE (IOP) AND FOLLOW-UP DATA

Category[a]	No. of Eyes	Average Prelaser IOP (mm Hg)	Average Postlaser IOP (mm Hg)	Average △ IOP (mm Hg)	Average Follow-up (mo)
All eyes	300	24.1	17.0	−7.1	5.0
Successful eyes	253	24.0	15.3	−8.7	5.5
Phakic eyes	263	24.4	16.8	−7.6	5.2
Aphakic eyes	37	22.3	19.5	−2.8	3.2
Primary OAG[a]	237	23.0	16.0	−6.4	5.0
Phakic primary OAG	208	23.4	16.4	−7.0	5.2
Aphakic primary OAG	29	21.7	19.6	−2.1	2.7
Pseudoexfoliation glaucoma	34	28.5	16.1	−12.4	5.0
Pigmentary glaucoma	6	25.0	15.0	−10.0	13.5
Angle-recession glaucoma	4	21.8	16.8	−5.0	8.7
Glaucoma secondary to uveitis	4	35.5	23.7	−11.8	4.3

[a]OAG = open-angle glaucoma.

and follow-up data for the major categories of eyes treated are given in Table 2. Table 3 summarizes tonographic data in categories of eyes in which reliable curves were available. Table 4 notes the number of eyes classified as failures and successes and gives the percentage of successfully treated eyes in each major category.

Phakic vs. Aphakic Eyes

Laser trabeculoplasty prevented glaucoma surgery in 85 percent of phakic eyes. In general, most aphakic eyes responded less well to trabeculoplasty than phakic eyes, however, individual eyes responded quite well.

TABLE 3. TONOGRAPHY DATA

Category	No. of Eyes	Average Prelaser C[a] (μ1/min/mm Hg)	Average Postlaser C (μ1/min/mm Hg)	Average △ C (μ1/min/mm Hg)
All eyes	173	0.14	0.23	+0.09
Successful eyes	163	0.10	0.23	+0.13
Phakic eyes	154	0.13	0.23	+0.10
Aphakic eyes	19	0.15	0.22	+0.07
Primary OAG	141	0.15	0.24	+0.09
Phakic primary OAG	127	0.15	0.24	+0.09
Aphakic primary OAG	15	0.17	0.23	+0.06
Pseudoexfoliation glaucoma	20	0.08	0.18	+0.10
Pigmentary glaucoma	5	0.08	0.19	+0.11
Glaucoma secondary to uveitis	1	0.08	0.16	+0.08

[a] C = the facility of outflow; OAG = open-angle glaucoma.

TABLE 4. SUCCESS RATES

Category	No. of Eyes	No. of Failure Eyes	No. of Successful Eyes	Success (%)
All eyes	300	47	253	84.3
Phakic eyes	263	33	230	87.5
Aphakic eyes	37	14	23	62.1
Primary OAG[a]	237	35	202	85.2
Phakic primary OAG	208	23	185	88.9
Aphakic primary OAG	29	12	17	58.6
Pseudoexfoliation glaucoma	34	1	33	97.1
Pigmentary glaucoma	6	0	6	100
Angle-recession glaucoma	4	1	3	75
Glaucoma secondary to uveitis	4	1	3	75

[a]OAG = open-angle glaucoma.

Among the 37 aphakic eyes in our series, we avoided performing surgery in 23 (62.1 percent).

Eyes with Partially Closed Angles

We treated with laser trabeculoplasty 17 eyes where the angle was partially closed with peripheral anterior synechiae. Nine (52.9 percent) of these eyes had successful results. In these 9, an average of 6½ clock hours of open angle were available for treatment, and an average of 54 laser spots were placed on the available trabecular meshwork in each eye. The average prelaser IOP in these 9 eyes was 19.8 mm Hg, and the average IOP reduction obtained after laser trabeculoplasty was 4.12 mm Hg (average follow-up period, 4.1 months). Four of the nine eyes had tonographic data available. The average prelaser values were C = 0.14, Po/C = 167, and the average postlaser values were C = 0.22, Po/C = 63.

Tapering of Medications

Tapering of glaucoma medications may be done judiciously when substantial reductions in IOP are noted after laser trabeculoplasty. In some patients, carbonic anhydrase inhibitors have been discontinued; in some others with cataracts and glaucoma, miotics have been discontinued because visual acuity had improved without their use. Despite tapering of medication in 30 percent of eyes, the IOP reduction remained sufficient to avoid glaucoma surgery. Medications should be tapered only if a substantial reduction of IOP has been obtained and if the patient appears

TABLE 5. AVERAGE △IOP^a IN RELATION TO AGE

Age (yr)	No. of Eyes	Average △ IOP (mm Hg)	No. of Failure Eyes	Successful Eyes (%)	Average Follow-up (mo)
≥ 40	278	−7.4	35	87.5	10.0
< 40	22	−1.4	12	45.5	6.3

^{a}Change in intraocular pressure (IOP) after trabeculoplasty.

overmedicated. Only one drug should be withdrawn at a time, and the IOP should be frequently monitored.

Age, Sex, and Race

Laser trabeculoplasty was more effective in patients 40 years of age or older (Table 5) and was equally effective in men and women (Table 6). Eyes of black patients were effectively treated with laser trabeculoplasty. Among ten eyes of nine black patients, trabeculoplasty prevented glaucoma surgery in seven eyes. The average prelaser IOP in these 7 eyes was 23.9 mm Hg, and the average reduction of IOP obtained after laser trabeculoplasty was 6.9 mm Hg (average follow-up period, 7.6 months).

Reduction of IOP

The average reduction of IOP obtained in successfully treated eyes did not diminish with time (Table 7), and was related to the average prelaser IOP. The higher the prelaser IOP, the greater the magnitude of pressure reduction obtained with the laser (Table 8).

Eyes with Previous Glaucoma Surgery

Thirty eyes with failed glaucoma surgical procedures were treated with laser trabeculoplasty. Seventeen (56.6 percent) were considered successes after laser trabeculoplasty because further glaucoma surgery was not necessary. Among these 17 eyes the average prelaser IOP was 25.1 mm Hg. The average IOP reduction after laser trabeculoplasty was 9.5 mm Hg (average follow-up period, 5.7 months). Laser trabeculoplasty was most

TABLE 6. AVERAGE △IOP^a IN RELATION TO SEX

	Eyes	(mm Hg)	No. of Failure Eyes	Successful Eyes (%)	Average Follow-up (mo)
Males	144	−7.1	22	85.0	6.0
Females	156	−7.0	25	84.0	4.5

^{a}Change in intraocular pressure (IOP) after trabeculoplasty.

TABLE 7. AVERAGE △IOP[a] IN RELATION TO LENGTH OF FOLLOW-UP IN SUCCESSFUL EYES

Length of Follow-up	No. of Eyes	Average △IOP (mm Hg)
1 yr	19	−7.9
9 mo to 1 yr	32	−8.8
6 mo to < 9 mo	39	−9.9
3 mo to < 6 mo	89	−8.6
2 mo to < 3 mo	24	−7.8
1 mo to < 2 mo	37	−7.9

[a]Change in intraocular pressure (IOP) after trabeculoplasty.

effective in phakic eyes that had filtering surgery and was least effective in aphakic eyes that had failed cyclodialysis.

Cataract Extraction after Trabeculoplasty

Five eyes in our series underwent intracapsular cataract extraction after IOP control was achieved with laser trabeculoplasty. Four of these eyes had completely open angles before trabeculoplasty. Our data indicated that good pressure control persisted in these eyes after cataract extraction despite tapering of medications. In all four eyes, the IOP reduction obtained with trabeculoplasty appeared to be enhanced further after cataract extraction (Table 9). The number of eyes that underwent cataract extraction after trabeculoplasty was too small to delineate the optimal time for cataract extraction after trabeculoplasty. The average interval of time in our series was approximately 5 months. Wise[13] believes that cataract extraction may be done 6 weeks after trabeculoplasty.

Retreatment of Eyes

Our experience with retreatment of eyes with laser trabeculoplasty was limited. We retreated the entire circumference of the trabecular meshwork in three eyes. In two of these, no lasting reduction of IOP was

TABLE 8. AVERAGE △IOP[a] IN RELATION TO PRELASER IOP IN SUCCESSFUL EYES

Prelaser IOP (mm Hg)	No. of Eyes	Average △ IOP (mm Hg)	Average FU[b] (mo)	IOP Reduction (%)
≥ 50	3	−25.0	4.8	50.0
≥ 40 to 49	6	−21.3	6.5	47.3
≥ 30 to 39	45	−13.9	5.5	39.7
≥ 20 to 29	134	−7.6	6.0	30.4
≥ 10 to 19	65	−4.2	4.7	28.0

[a]Change in intraocular pressure (IOP) after trabeculoplasty.
[b]FU = follow-up.

TABLE 9. EFFECT OF INTRACAPSULAR CATARACT EXTRACTION ON △IOP OB-
TAINED WITH TRABECULOPLASTY (4 EYES)[a]

Eye	Pre-laser IOP (mm Hg)	Post-laser IOP (mm Hg)	△ IOP Before CE[b] (mm Hg)	△ IOP After CE[c] (mm Hg)	Length of FU[d] Between Laser CE (mo)	Length of FU After CE (mo)	Taperings of Medication
1	30	22	−8.0	−7.0	8.0	5.0	Yes
2	30	23	−7.0	−14.0	7.5	7.0	No
3	24	17	−7.0	−2.0	2.5	6.2	Yes
4	19	15	−4.0	−1.0	1.7	6.0	Yes
AVERAGE	25.8	19.3	−6.5	−6.0	5.0	6.0	

[a]Eyes with 360° open angles.
[b]Cataract extraction.
[c]IOP just prior to cataract extraction compared to afternoon IOP measured at end of follow-up period.
[d]FU = follow-up.

obtained and both had to undergo surgery and were classified as failures. In the remaining eye, which had phakic open-angle glaucoma, the IOP reduction was 5 mm Hg for a 3-week follow-up period after retreatment. Unfortunately, the patient was lost to follow-up. The safety and efficacy of retreatment have not been determined as yet.

Trabeculoplasty Combined with Gonioplasty and Iridotomy

We found no adverse effect on IOP reduction when two other types of anterior segment laser procedures (i.e., gonioplasty and iridotomy) were performed in conjunction with laser trabeculoplasty.

Gonioplasty was very useful in widening the inlet of a narrow angle, allowing a clear view of the trabecular meshwork to make laser trabeculoplasty feasible. In 36 eyes in which gonioplasty was done at the same sitting just before trabeculoplasty, an average IOP reduction of 8.7 mm Hg has been maintained for an average follow-up period of 5 months.

Three eyes in our series with closeable angles had laser iridotomies performed prior to trabeculoplasty. In two eyes, the iridotomy was done a few days before trabeculoplasty and in one the iridotomy was performed at the same sitting just before trabeculoplasty. All three eyes have maintained an average IOP reduction of 8.6 mm Hg for an average follow-up period of 10 months.

COMPLICATIONS

Iritis

The iritis we have seen generally has been mild and transient. It usually lasts for less than 1 week after trabeculoplasty and is easily controlled with topical steroids.

Hemorrhage

In 7 of 300 (2.3 percent) eyes in our series, a small amount of bleeding occurred from the trabecular meshwork during treatment. Two different patterns of hemorrhage were observed. Usually, the onset of hemorrhage was sudden, the blood appeared to come directly from the area of the meshwork where the laser spot has been applied, and bleeding occurred immediately after laser application. Occasionally, blood oozed from the trabecular meshwork from areas adjacent to the spots. The occurrence of hemorrhage does not have a long-term adverse effect on IOP reduction or on the facility of outflow.

This type of bleeding is thought to be a reflux of blood from Schlemm's canal, although its occurrence does not correlate with the presence of blood in Schlemm's canal before trabeculoplasty. The presence of blood in Schlemm's canal prior to trabeculoplasty is not a contraindication to treatment.

If bleeding from the trabecular meshwork occurs during trabeculoplasty, one can first try to tamponade it by applying moderate pressure on the globe with the Goldmann goniocontact lens. In the past when bleeding persisted, it was stopped with relatively large-sized laser spots of low power. Often less than five applications were required to stop the bleeding.

More recently, we have found that if the bleeding does not stop when moderate pressure is applied on the globe with the Goldmann lens, it will almost always stop if the lens is removed from the eye or if the lens is drawn toward the surgeon to eliminate all compression of the episcleral veins by the lens. We now believe that the application of laser spots to the point of bleeding is unnecessary in most eyes.

Peripheral Anterior Synechiae

Gonioscopic examination was performed in 70 eyes several weeks to months after trabeculoplasty. In 33 (47.1 percent) of these eyes, peripheral anterior synechiae were seen. Although the incidence seems high, it should be noted that, in general, these were tiny, peaked synechiae to the level of the scleral spur and ciliary body band. Only 9 of the 33 eyes had synechiae present to the level of the trabecular meshwork and all 9 showed good improvement in facility of outflow and good reduction of IOP. It seems logical that the formation of peripheral anterior synechiae would occur more frequently with use of high energy levels and in eyes with angles with narrow inlets. However, in analyzing our data, we were unable to find a positive correlation between formation of synechiae and high energy levels or pretreatment width of the angle.

Elevation of IOP

The most serious potential complication of laser trabeculoplasty is post-treatment elevation of IOP.[12,14] The mechanism of this rise of pressure is unclear. It does not correlate with the presence of iritis. It is usually

transient, and it is associated with a temporary decrease in the facility of outflow.

Among our 300 eyes treated, elevations ranging from 1 mm Hg above prelaser IOP were seen in 76 (25.3 percent) eyes. We noted that the peaks of these pressure elevations generally occurred in the first 3 weeks after treatment. Only 10 percent of the eyes that showed pressure elevation had increases exceeding prelaser IOPs by more than 15 mm Hg.

Among the initial 100 eyes that were considered to be successfully treated with laser trabeculoplasty, 21 showed transient pressure rises ranging from 1 to 19 mm Hg above baseline. Table 10 indicates when the peaks of these pressure elevations were measured and the average increase in pressure above baseline. The occurrence of these pressure elevations does not reflect failure of laser trabeculoplasty. It should be noted that good reductions in IOP were observed in these same 21 eyes several months after laser trabeculoplasty.

From these data, we believe that a decision on surgical intervention should be delayed, if at all possible, if an elevation of IOP is noted after treatment. We recognize that in some eyes with severe glaucomatous cupping and field loss, it may not be safe to wait for this length of time. That these pressure elevations can occur demands that patients be followed up very carefully and frequently during the first few weeks after laser therapy.

Loss of Central Vision Secondary to IOP Elevation

Loss of central vision due to a temporary posttreatment rise in IOP was seen in one eye in our series. The patient was an 83-year-old man with phakic primary open-angle glaucoma who had 20/200 vision with a totally cupped disc and a small central island on visual field testing. His prelaser IOP was 30 mm Hg. Trabeculoplasty was done with 100 spots being applied to the entire circumference of the trabecular meshwork at one session. Three days later, his IOP was 42 mm Hg and his vision had decreased to counting fingers at 1 foot. Ironically, 7 weeks after trabeculoplasty, the IOP in the treated eye was 10 mm Hg.

We noted these posttreatment pressure elevations relatively early in

TABLE 10. SUCCESSFUL EYES WITH IOP ELEVATION AFTER LASER TRABECULOPLASTY (21 EYES)

No. of Eyes	Time after Laser Treatment	Average Increase in IOP (Compared to Prelaser IOP)	Average Follow-up (mo)	Decrease in IOP (Compared to Prelaser IOP)
4	1–3 days	+8.5 mm Hg	11.8	−9.3 mm Hg
5	4–6 days	+9.6 mm Hg	10.2	−8.4 mm Hg
8	1–<2 weeks	+5.6 mm Hg	8.3	−6.5 mm Hg
4	2–<3 weeks	+11.7 mm Hg	7.5	−6.3 mm Hg

our experience with trabeculoplasty. In an attempt to find ways to prevent this rise in pressure, we started in March 1980 to treat some eyes with 50 spots at each of two treatment sessions.

Of the 283 eyes in our series with completely open angles, 139 were treated with 100 burns applied to the entire circumference of the trabecular meshwork at one treatment session and 102 eyes were treated with 50 burns applied to one-half of the circumference (180 degrees) of the trabecular meshwork at each of two treatment sessions separated by a few days to several weeks. The average length of time between sessions was 3.5 weeks. Table 11 indicates average IOP reduction, percent success, and the incidence and degree of pressure elevations in the two groups.

The reduction of IOP between the two groups was not statistically significant using a one-tailed t-test ($p > 0.5$). The percentage of eyes successfully treated in each group was similar. The percentage of eyes that showed elevated pressures after trabeculoplasty was also similar for both groups. The main difference between the two groups was that eyes treated at one treatment session more frequently had pressure elevations 5 and 10 mm Hg exceeding prelaser IOPs than eyes treated at two sessions.

At present, we recommend that all eyes with marked glaucomatous damage of the optic nerves be treated in two treatment sessions. For those in which the angle is partially closed with peripheral anterior synechia, it is probably safe to treat half of the available trabecular meshwork at each of two treatment sessions.

During the course of treating eyes in two sessions we found that 40 eyes responded very well to treatment of only one-half of the angle. We have not yet treated the remaining half of the angle in these eyes because they have shown an average pressure reduction of 8.2 mm Hg and improved facility of outflow (average follow-up period, 3 months).

TABLE 11. COMPARISON OF ONE TREATMENT SESSION AND TWO TREATMENT SESSIONS

	One Treatment Session (139 eyes)	Two Treatment Sessions (102 eyes)
Average IOP after treatment (mm Hg)	−7.8	−6.3
Success (%)	84.9	86.3
	(118/139 eyes)	(88/102 eyes)
Eyes with elevated IOP after treatment (%)	25.2	25.4
	(35/139 eyes)	(26/102 eyes)
Eyes with IOP elevation 5 mm Hg above baseline (%)	42.9	65.4
	(15/35 eyes)	(17/26 eyes)
Eyes with IOP elevation 5 mm Hg above baseline (%)	57.1	34.6
	(20/35 eyes)	(9/26 eyes)
Eyes with IOP elevation 10 mm Hg above baseline (%)	37.1	11.5
	(13/35 eyes)	(3/26 eyes)

At the present time, we routinely treat only one-half of the angle. If satisfactory pressure reduction is obtained, we do not treat the remaining half. If pressure reduction is inadequate, the remainder is treated.

A significant finding in our study is that it is possible to make glaucoma worse with laser trabeculoplasty. If we define a worsening glaucoma as a persistent elevation of IOP of 5 mm Hg or more above baseline that does not return to baseline levels before surgical intervention, glaucoma was made worse in 10 of 300 (3 percent) eyes in our series. Seven of these ten eyes were phakic with primary open-angle glaucoma. Therefore, all patients should receive a trial of maximally tolerated medical therapy before trabeculoplasty is performed.

Further investigation is needed to answer many remaining questions. Although pressure elevations can occur after treatment and the procedure can make glaucoma worse in a small percentage of eyes, laser trabeculoplasty has proved to be an extremely useful therapeutic modality in lowering IOP to levels sufficient to avoid surgical intervention.

REFERENCES

1. Krasnov MM: Laseropuncture of anterior chamber angle in glaucoma. Am J Ophthalmol 75:674, 1973
2. Worthen DM, Wickham MG. Argon laser trabeculotomy. Trans Am Acad Ophthalmol Otolaryngol 78:37, 1974
3. Wickham MG, Worthen DM: Argon laser trabeculotomy long term follow up. Ophthalmology 86:495, 1979
4. Teichmann I, Teichmann KD, Fechner PUL: Glaucoma operation with argon laser. EENT Mon 55:209, 1976
5. Ticho U, Zauberman H: Argon laser application to the angle structures in the glaucomas. Arch Ophthalmol 94:61, 1976
6. Wise JB, Witter SL: Argon laser therapy for open angle glaucoma: A pilot study. Arch Ophthalmol 97:319, 1979
7. Wise JB: Long term control of adult open angle glaucoma by argon laser treatment. Ophthalmology 88:197, 1981
8. Schwartz AL, Whitten ME, Bleiman B, et al: Argon laser trabecular surgery in uncontrolled phakic open angle glaucoma. Ophthalmology 88:203, 1981
9. Wilensky JT, Jampol LM: Laser therapy for open angle glaucoma. Ophthalmology 88:213, 1981
10. Thomas JV, Simmons RJ, Belcher CD: Argon laser trabeculoplasty in the management of the pre-surgical glaucoma patient. Ophthalmology 89:187, 1982
11. Simmons, RJ, Thomas JV, Belcher CD, et al: Argon laser trabeculoplasty in the management of phakic and aphakic glaucoma. Presented at the National Society for the Prevention of Blindness Symposium on Glaucoma. Atlanta, Georgia, November 1–6, 1981
12. Thomas, JV, Simmons RJ, Belcher CD: Complications of argon laser trabeculoplasty. Glaucoma 4:50, 1982

13. Simmons RJ, Thomas JV, Dueker D, et al: Round Table Discussion on Laser Trabeculoplasty, Ophthalmic Forum 1(2):39, 1983.
14. Thomas JV, Simmons RJ: Management of complications of laser trabeculoplasty. Unpublished data, 1983

Complications

Marc F. Lieberman

The data presented were gathered from a series of patients (Table 1) treated by Drs. D. Hoskins and J. Hetherington in San Francisco.[1] The 142 eyes of 112 patients were divided into two categories: those that have had some form of prior surgery and those that have not. The follow-up period has been from 9 to 18 months (average, 12 months). The standard parameters of ocular health have been monitored, with the proviso that in a large referral-type practice some data are not retrievable.

Our primary focus during this pilot study was on the intraocular pressure (IOP) response to laser treatment. Medications were adjusted according to patient needs and were not held constant. At the time, the standard trabeculoplasty technique consisted of the following parameters: 85 to 110 applications of argon energy; 0.1-second duration 50-μ sized spots placed above the junction of the scleral spur and trabecular meshwork; and power settings of 750 to 1100 mW (Coherent model 900). We used the minimal amount of energy needed to blanch tissue. The entire angle circumference was treated, as visualized with a single-mirror Goldmann goniolens. Burns to the peripheral iris were used infrequently to expose inaccessible angle structures.

Our classification of patients and overall pressure results are shown in Tables 2 and 3. In brief, chronic open-angle glaucoma (COAG) patients, without prior surgery, showed an average pressure decrease of 8 mm Hg. Patients with pigmentary dispersion and pseudoexfoliation glaucoma showed similar favorable responses; those with uveitis and angle-recession glaucoma failed despite the presence of open angles. Eyes that had surgery prior to the trabeculoplasty were less predictable, though the following trend was noted: with just one procedure before trabeculoplasty—e.g., laser iridotomy or cataract extraction—the IOP response was only slightly less (5 mm Hg decrease) than in nonoperated eyes. Those with more than one surgery did less well. Nearly every category had a tremendous spread of responses: from a +3 to a −25 mm Hg change.

With our moderate-term follow-up period and large series, we have been able to sketch the limitations of laser trabeculoplasty. Most findings will be confined to the experience of 71 patients whose 99 eyes had COAG, exclusive of traumatic and uveitic diatheses. When we began our

TABLE 1. LASER TRABECULOPLASTY STUDY DATA[a]

Classification of Patients			
No Prior Surgery	*No. of Patients (No. of Eyes)*	*Previous Surgery*	*No. of Patients (No. of Eyes)*
Chronic open-angle glaucoma	55 (76)	Glaucoma surgery	16 (17)
Pigment disperson syndrome	10 (16)	Aphakia	9 (10)
Exfoliation syndrome	6 (7)	Goniodysgenesis	7 (7)
Trauma/uveitis	6 (9)		

[a]A total of 112 patients (142 eyes) were followed from 9 to 27 months (average, 12 months).

series, we heeded a quote Dr. Robert Shaffer is fond of recalling: "Let's use this new technique while it still works great and has no complications." "Complications" is too strong a word because it conjures up images of things going awry, undermining the end result. My preference is to discuss the drawbacks of laser trabeculoplasty since the hoped-for decrease in IOP was usually obtained, though not without other associated events. As we use this new therapy, the important thing is that we be mindful of what to look for and what we and our patients can expect.

The single most common drawback to laser trabeculoplasty is an *IOP elevation* in the first few hours after treatment. With the assistance of Dr. Donald Minckler, the San Francisco group did serial pressure checks over the first 24 hours in 106 laser trabeculoplasty patients. Exactly one-third of these patients showed pressure rises of more than 5 mm Hg—two thirds of these pressure spikes were greater than 10 mm Hg over baseline levels (Table 4). This spike phenomenon was generally restricted to the first day of treatment.

When 49 different patients had tension checks 24 hours after laser trabeculoplasty, only 3 had pressures greater than baseline (Table 4). All

TABLE 2. RESPONSIVENESS TO LASER TRABECULOPLASTY IN UNOPERATED EYES

Diagnosis	No. of Eyes	Failures	Average Preoperative IOP[a] (mm Hg)	Average Reduction in IOP (mm Hg)	No. of Eyes Using Medication		
					Less	*Same*	*More*
Chronic open-angle glaucoma	76	14	26	8	34	21	2
Pigment disperson syndrome	16	5	26	8.5	8	3	—
Exfoliation syndrome	7	2	31	14	3	2	—
Trauma/uveitis	9	7	27	4	—	—	—

[a]IOP = intraocular pressure.

TABLE 3. RESPONSIVENESS TO LASER TRABECULOPLASTY IN PREVIOUSLY OPERATED EYES

Diagnosis	No. of Eyes	Failures	Average Preoperative IOP[a] (mm Hg)	Average Reduction in IOP[a] (mm Hg)	No. of Eyes Using Medication		
					Less	Same	More
Phakic filter	10	3	28	10	2	3	2
Aphakic filter	5	2	25	5	1	2	—
Iridectomy	4	0	29	9	2	2	—
Aphakia	7	1	21	5	4	2	—
Goniotomy/ trabeculotomy	3	2	26	12	1	—	—

[a]IOP = intraocular pressure.

of these patients, as well as our 71 COAGs were already receiving maximally tolerated medical therapy. None were given steroid drops or aspirin before the laser treatment. This means that one of every five patients treated can expect a significant early IOP elevation.

A similar but more impressive increase in IOP is seen immediately after laser iridotomy. In a control series of 19 patients, 8 had elevations of more than 10 mm Hg. With laser trabeculoplasty, we can imagine that focal edema in the outflow path that the laser energy causes resolves in a matter of hours, so that drainage resumes. But the iridotomy experience suggests an acute inflammatory component. Insofar as there is little, if any, dispersal of tissue debris with laser trabeculoplasty as there is with iridotomy, a humoral mechanism is suspected. Underway now are studies of the effect of pretreatment prostaglandin and inflammatory inhibitors and on variations in treatment protocols.

The practical aspects of this increase in pressure are three: (1) that patients should be maintained on their maximal regimen for treatment; (2) that laser treatment be done early in the day so pressures can be monitored; and (3) that symptoms of corneal edema or amaurosis be

TABLE 4. ACUTE INTRAOCULAR PRESSURE (IOP) CHANGES AFTER LASER TRABECULOPLASTY

IOP (mm Hg)	IOP Measured During First 6 Hr (n = 106 eyes): No. of Eyes	Measured at Day 1 (n = 49 eyes): No. of Eyes
Reduction ≥ 5	24	29
Same ± 4	46	17
Increased ≥ 5	36	3
5–9	15	—
10–20	11	2
> 20	10	1

explained and that osmotic agents be available. Although the pressure spike rapidly tapers within 24 hours, tensions may fluctuate during the next 3 weeks and not settle down to their eventual level for 4 to 6 weeks. We therefore wait at least 6 weeks before concluding if the laser treatment worked.

The *inflammatory sequelae* of nongranulomatous iritis and low anterior synechiae have been insignificant in our series. Anterior chamber ray and cell persist at low levels for the first 10 days and usually taper by the third week. "Ciliary synechiae"—that is, discrete, nonconfluent foci or iris adhesions below or at the scleral spur that obscure a gonioscopic view of the ciliary body but not the filtering structures (as implied by "peripheral anterior synechiae [PAS]")—developed in approximately 15 percent of our patients. These did not progress to classic PAS; they involved less than a total of two clock hours of the angle; and they were more likely to occur in angles classified as less than Grade II (Shaffer classification) or in angles whose peripheral irides were intentionally or accidentally treated.

Another drawback in predicting the laser effect was the surprising *asymmetric response* between two fellow eyes. Differences were found in the timing and extent of pressure elevations in the early posttreatment period, in the final amount of pressure reduction, in field and acuity stability, and in the duration and severity of iritis. One patient, for example, showed a mild, uncomplicated pressure elevation from 28 to 33 mm Hg in the first week. When her second eye was treated 6 months later, the pressure rose from 24 to 45 mm Hg and resulted in corneal edema. A second patient who underwent bilateral treatment had a pressure decrease in one eye of 5 mm Hg with stable field and acuity after 1½ years of follow-up, yet sustained a significant, unexplained decrease in acuity in the fellow eye, whose pressure had been lowered to 21 mm Hg.

Unpredictable too were the responses to a second laser trabeculoplasty in a previously treated eye. Retreatment was done in ten eyes of nine patients, but a follow-up of more than 6 months is available in only three. All three patients began with pretreatment IOP in the mid-30s; 6 months after the first 100-burn treatment, IOP was lowered to the upper-20s. A second full treatment of 100 burns reduced IOP in only one of these eyes. By and large, the San Francisco group believes a second full laser trabeculoplasty is not useful.

An infrequent but truly serious finding in our series was the *deterioration of visual field* despite a good pressure response. In the 54 eyes whose Goldmann visual fields were performed by the same technicians before and after laser trabeculoplasty, 9 developed either significant deepening (more than 1.0 log unit) of extant scotomata or new scotomata, only 1 of which could possibly be ascribed to worsening of cataract. (Of peripheral interest are four patients who showed improvement of their fields, unrelated to change in miotic therapy.)

The actual timing of the field deterioration remains unclear; visual

fields were done on a standard 6- and 12-month schedule. It is easy to imagine that an early posttreatment pressure spike could adversely affect an already damaged and marginal optic nerve; or perhaps the lability of tensions in the first 3 to 6 weeks acts as several subacute insults. (Although I am assuming a direct relationship between IOP and nerve damage, I suppose indirect and obscure laser or toxic effects could be postulated.)

Because the patients in this study were otherwise surgical candidates, having either progressive glaucomatous atrophy or inadequate medical control of their IOP, the progression of field defects after laser trabeculo-plasty, despite good pressure control, is not entirely unexpected. In an important study by Werner and coworkers,[2] 10 of 24 eyes showed signifi-cant field progression after "successful" (i.e., pressure-lowering) trabecu-lectomies. They concluded that prognosis depended on a constant control of IOP fluctuations—a state not always achieved by either laser or filter-ing surgery.

A number of our patients (7 of 54) showed *deterioration in visual acuity.* One case could be ascribed to cataract, which may or may not be related to laser surgery (I doubt it). Unfortunately some of these patients did not have repeated refractions on returning to their referring physicians within the follow-up interval. No case of cystoid macular edema, ischemic optic neuropathy, or direct macular burn, however, was seen in our series.

The *exacerbation of glaucoma* by laser trabeculoplasty is a controversial issue to be considered. Monkeys have been treated using the same pa-rameters as our patients, except for a 0.5 instead of 0.1-second duration and the outflow facility was severely reduced, thus creating an experimen-tal glaucoma. Can laser trabeculoplasty make an open-angle glaucoma worse or more resistant to therapy?

In 21 of 99 eyes in our series with open-angle glaucoma, laser trabe-culoplasty "failed" in the sense that the responsible surgeon did not deem the resultant pressure safe for the eye, and either repeated treatment or filtering surgery was necessary. In these patients, who were taken out of the study anywhere from 3 weeks to 15 months (but usually in the first 12 weeks) after treatment, their glaucoma can be said to have been exacer-bated in that their damaged nerves were exposed to inadequate control for some duration. If a stricter definition of exacerbation is employed— that the glaucoma was made more difficult to manage because of laser therapy—then only 2 of the remaining 78 eyes could be classified as having been exacerbated. These two eyes required more or stronger medications than before laser treatment. But no surgical result was influ-enced or biased by the laser therapy.

The list of theoretic drawbacks could be as long as the time needed to hypothesize them. Inadvertent laser burns to the cornea, lens, or retina could occur with bad luck or carelessness. Serious worsening of uveitis has been reported by others. My own preliminary data on aqueous fluoropho-tometry (facilitated by the laboratory of Norman Blair, M.D., University

of Illinois Eye and Ear Infirmary, Chicago) in three patients treated with laser trabeculoplasty suggest a disruption in the blood-aqueous barrier that persists well beyond the 2 to 3 weeks' time during which mild iritis can be detected at the slit lamp. The validity, not to mention significance, of this observation is speculative.

In summary, laser trabeculoplasty is a viable and valuable modality whose advantages and disadvantages lie somewhere between medical and surgical treatment for open-angle glaucoma. Benefits of the laser are similar to those of a strong topical medicine augmenting, but rarely replacing, medical therapy. Its complications, of fluctuating pressure levels and spikes, are more similar to the consequences of filtering surgery.

REFERENCES

1. Lieberman MF, Hogkins HD, Hetherington J: Laser trabeculoplasty and the glaucomas. Ophthalmology 90:790, 1983
2. Werner EB, Drance SM, Schulzer M: Trabeculectomy and the progression of glaucomatous visual field loss. Arch Ophthalmol 95:1374, 1977

CHAPTER 3

Photomydriasis and Coreopexy

Irvin P. Pollack

One interesting application of laser energy has been to alter the shape of the pupil. This approach can be used to enlarge the pupil in persons whose vision has been reduced by the extreme miosis induced by glaucoma medications. The blue-green argon laser beam is highly absorbed by iris tissues, especially by the pigment. On absorption, the continuous-wave argon laser beam is converted to heat, which produces a thermal burn at the treated site. If this burn is placed close enough to the pupil, it will shrink the iris tissue and deflect the pupil toward the treated site.[1]

One can enlarge the pupil by encircling it with a series 200 to 500 μ 500 coagulation spots for 0.1 to 0.2-second duration with a power of 200 to 600 mW (Fig. 1). These applications are made just outside the pupil and within the collarette of the iris. (*Editor's Note:* Photomydriasis can also be achieved by placing a double ring of burns in the iris just outside the collarette (Fig. 2). The burn parameters are similar to those used by Dr. Pollack.) They may be placed in a single or double row, depending on how much pupillary dilation is required. At the same time, one must be extremely careful that the beam does not enter the pupil and damage the posterior pole. To prevent this, the patient should fixate on a target to steady the eye, and great care must be exercised in the treatment. If the first treatment is insufficient, it can be repeated 2 or 3 weeks later in a similar manner. One may also extend the treatment into a third row, slightly more peripheral than the first two, to achieve better mydriasis.

Photomydriasis can widen the pupil and help to reduce the "darkness" that many patients complain about after instilling miotics. Candi-

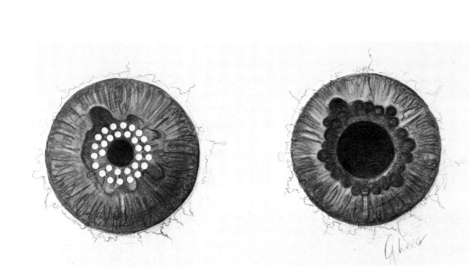

Figure 1. A series of continuous laser burns encircle the pupil. These thermal coagulations contract the tissue and enlarge the pupillary space.

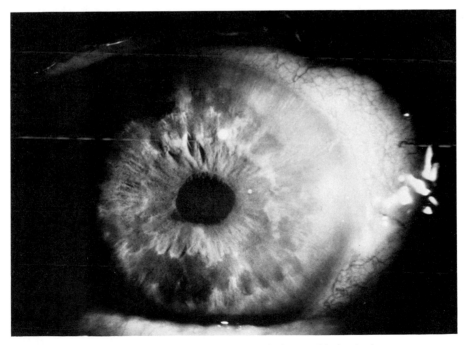

Figure 2. Photograph of an eye that has had photomydriasis; the burns were placed outside the collarette.

dates for this therapy should be tested by dilating their pupil with a drop of phenylephrine hydrochloride (Neo-Synephrine) to see if the acuity or brightness of vision improves. If it does, then photomydriasis may be indicated. Finally, in some cases, photomydriasis may make it easier to examine the posterior pole.

Photomydriasis does not have a 100 percent success rate. In some patients the beneficial widening of the pupil decreases after several days to weeks, and the pupil may return to its pretreatment size. Also, if posterior synechiae are present—and this is a frequent complication of long-term miotic therapy—the pupil may dilate irregularly or it may not dilate at all. In some patients with extremely miotic pupils, this laser treatment will scatter iris pigment into the pupil and may actually make the vision worse.

One can also use photomydriasis to deflect an updrawn pupil in an aphakic eye (Fig. 3). A single or double row of laser burns is placed around the lower part of the updrawn pupil in an attempt to pull the pupillary space closer to the visual axis.

Laser iridotomy is now widely employed to treat pupillary block angle-closure glaucoma. However, when the anterior chamber is extremely shallow, it may be difficult to produce a laser iridotomy to break the pupillary block. The cornea may be so close to the iris that laser treatment to the iris produces a thermal burn on the corneal endothelium. In our experience, a weak laser burn in the peripheral iris will tighten the dilator muscle and deepen the chamber at that point. One can then use a series of stronger burns to complete an iridotomy. If this fails, or as an alternative, one can deflect the iris in one spot in an attempt to break the pupillary block. This will be successful only if the pupil can be drawn in such a manner that the posterior chamber pressure can overcome the block at the point of pupil deflection.

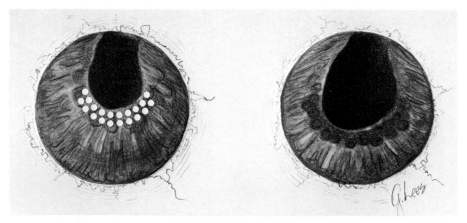

Figure 3. A row of laser burns placed along the lower border of an updrawn pupil can pull the pupil downward.

Photomydriasis may be used in a similar way in treating vitreous block glaucoma. In such cases, one may open the pupil sufficiently to break the vitreous block of the pupil or break the posterior synechiae between the pupil and vitreous face. The thermal effect can burn a hole through the vitreous face, allowing aqueous humor to resume its flow through the pupil.

After photomydriasis, the patient should continue to use the glaucoma medication. In addition, we prescribe topical prednisolone 1 percent, four times daily for 4 days.

The complications of photomydriasis can include iritis, pigment dispersion, increased intraocular pressure during the postoperative period, and accidental retinal burn. These complications are the same as those of laser iridotomy and trabeculoplasty. The amount of iritis and pigment dispersion that occurs is directly related to the amount of laser energy delivered to the iris. As with laser iridotomy, there is immediate dispersion of pigment and iris debris into the anterior chamber, and this effect is greater when more energy is used. After several hours the pigment and debris settle into the inferior angle, although some may also be seen on the corneal endothelial surface inferiorly.

James and coworkers[1] have shown in rabbit eyes that photomydriasis occurs with laser ablation of the iris sphincter. In addition, shrinkage of the dilator muscle fibers may be important to produce deflection of the pupil.[1]

Photomydriasis has a definite place in the treatment of glaucoma in suitable cases. However, it must be used judiciously because the laser beam must be directed very close to the pupil. Unfortunately, some of the cases that are most in need of treatment respond poorly, often because of previously formed posterior synechiae. Taking all of these factors into account, photomydriasis should be considered as still another way that laser energy can be used to treat glaucoma.

REFERENCE

1. James WA Jr, DeRoetth A Jr, Forbes M, et al: Argon laser photomydriasis. Am J Ophthalmolol 81:62, 1976

CHAPTER 4

Gonioplasty (Iridoretraction)

Richard J. Simmons and Omah S. Singh

Gonioplasty (iridoretraction) is a technique in which the argon laser is used to change the configuration of the peripheral iris. This is accomplished by applying low energy burns to the peripheral iris that are sufficient to contract the iris and widen the anterior chamber angle (Fig. 1). In addition, early peripheral anterior synechiae can frequently be broken or retracted by the technique. Based on our observations of the effects produced by this procedure in some of our patients, we began to use it in our practice in 1975,[1,2] but later discovered prior mention of this principle in reports by others.[3-6] Since that time, we have used and refined the technique and have extended its uses. In conjunction with other treatment modalities, it has proved effective in the treatment of selected cases of subacute and chronic primary angle-closure glaucoma, nanophthalmos, plateau iris configuration, neovascular glaucoma, and as an adjunct to laser trabeculoplasty in some cases of open-angle glaucoma.[1]

TECHNIQUE

Topical anesthetic drops are administered to the eye to be treated, and the patient is positioned at the argon laser slit lamp. Laser burns are applied to the peripheral iris either with or without (Figs. 2A and 2B) a mirrored goniolens, such as the Goldmann model. The technique requires low power settings, a moderately long exposure time, and a large spot size. We currently find the following parameters to be most effective:

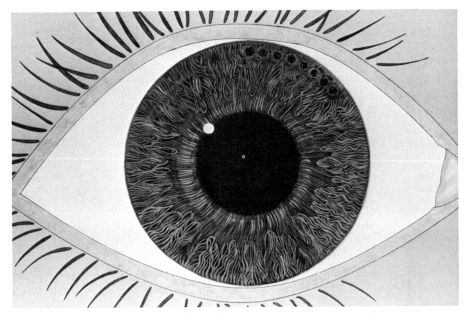

Figure 1. Laser burns are applied to the peripheral iris stroma in a localized area of treatment—one or two quadrants for subacute or chronic angle closure with only one or two clock hours of extreme narrowness and iris apposition. (*From Simmons RJ, Kimbrough RL, Belcher CD, et al: Transactions of the New Orleans Ophthalmological Society, St. Louis, CV Mosby, 1981.*[1])

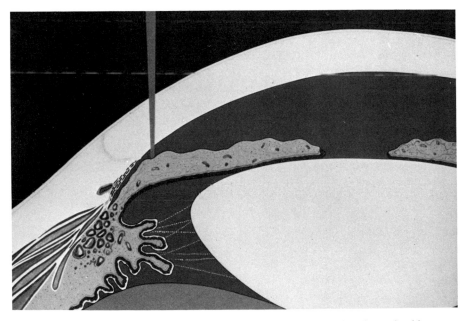

Figure 2.A. Laser burns of low energy levels are applied directly to the iris without a mirrored lens or a contact lens. (*From Simmons RJ, Kimbrough RL, Belcher CD, et al.*[1])

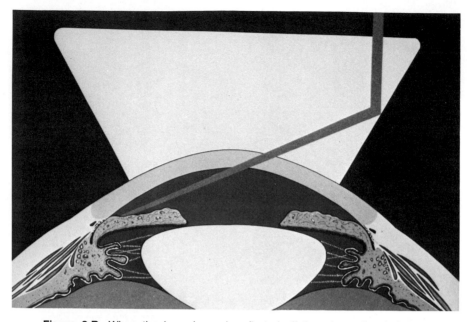

Figure 2.B. When the laser beam is reflected off the mirror of a goniolens, treatment can be applied more peripherally to detach synechiae. Higher energy levels are used than those required for the technique shown in **A.** (*From Simmons RJ, Kimbrough RL, Belcher CD, et al.*[1])

an initial power range of 100 to 200 mW (increasing the power if necessary), a large spot size (200 to 250 μ), and an exposure time of 0.2 second. The burns are placed on the iris, around the periphery just inside the arcus, so that the laser is directed through clear cornea (Fig. 1). This produces a distinct, apparent stromal burn that contracts and visibly flattens the iris immediately around the burn site. In some cases, early peripheral anterior synechiae are completely retracted by this process.

This technique is a gentle one; when properly applied, it involves no explosion or pigment dispersion, no lens opacity, and no distortion of the pupil. The technique applies just enough heat energy to the anterior iris stroma to contract its collagen and change its configuration (Fig. 3). The effect of the laser is immediately visible; when a mirrored goniolens is used, the surgeon can monitor the extent each laser application opens the angle. Normally, we prefer to treat the narrowest portion of the angle, so that it is moderately, but definitely, open. We avoid severe contracture, which may widen the angle to the extreme and distort the iris, and deep penetration of the iris, as in a laser iridectomy. The changes in the configuration produced with this technique are usually permanent or long-lasting, but gonioplasty can be repeated if needed, sometimes even a year or two later.

In performing gonioplasty, we prefer to use a contact lens on the eye

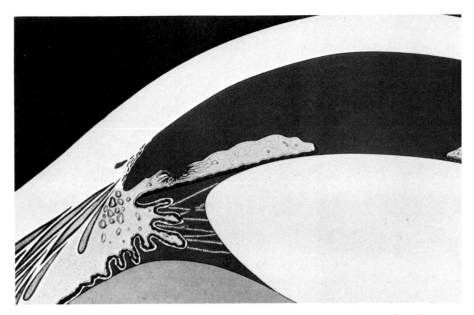

Figure 3. The extent of the burn is superficial, with resultant contraction of the iris stroma. Perforation is not desirable. (*From Simmons RJ, Kimbrough RL, Belcher CD, et al.*[1])

to cool the cornea and to allow visualization of the angle during the course of treatment. We usually employ a Goldmann lens, with a low energy laser beam applied directly onto the peripheral iris through the center of the lens without the use of the mirror. The mirror is then used to observe the angle to ensure that the desired widening of the angle or stripping of synechiae has been achieved. When it is more convenient, or when synechiae or the angle configuration does not show improvement with treatment by the direct laser beam, indirect laser application is performed by adjusting the power settings to higher energy levels and bouncing the beam off the mirror into the angle. This technique allows treatment closer to the base of the iris, and in some cases it is more effective in stripping synechiae that are reluctant to pull away from the meshwork.

COMPLICATIONS

We have found that the complications of gonioplasty are generally mild and transient. Pupillary distortion may occur with excessive power settings, but usually the distortion is minimal and, at its most severe, does not produce changes that compromise the visual axis. In several patients, mild

iritis, with a few cells in the aqueous, has been noted following gonioplasty. These effects can be minimized by employing the lowest possible laser intensity necessary to produce the desired contracture of the iris surface, flattening of the iris configuration, and widening of the angle. If gonioplasty fails to widen the angle, alternate conventional means of therapy such as surgical or laser iridectomy should be employed.

DISCUSSION

Laser gonioplasty is less traumatic than iridectomy because the energy levels applied to the iris, the number of burns, and the total energy employed in gonioplasty are considerably less than those required for laser iridectomy. In many cases of narrow angle with near or complete closure, both a component of pupillary block and a structural, anatomic component contribute to the forward convexity of the iris with eventual closure. Frequently pupillary block is the more important of the two components, as in the case of ordinary primary acute angle closure. In other cases the anatomic component is very important, for example, in plateau iris, for which iridectomy will relieve the pupillary block but may not widen the angle at all. In some cases of subacute and chronic angle closure the anatomic component appears to be significant, because gonioplasty can be effective in relieving closure. It does not reverse the pupillary block component, but does alter the anatomic configuration of the narrow angle, which comprises the structural factor. The ability to modify and alter the anatomic curvature of the iris is the important function of gonioplasty.

Gonioplasty is often permanent; however, if convexity of the iris gradually reappears over a period of months, additional laser burns can be applied to the previously treated area or adjacent areas at follow-up visits. Our routine for follow-up commonly includes one visit per month for the first 3 months after treatment; if the angle appears stable, the follow-up visits are decreased to 3- to 4-month intervals. Gonioscopy, applanation tonometry, and sometimes goniophotographs are done at each follow-up visit. In addition, patients with primary angle-closure glaucoma undergo darkroom tests in the prone position every 3 to 6 months. After treatment, if the eye shows increased or recurrent convexity of the iris that threatens closure of the angle, then further gonioplasty may be performed.

SELECTED USES OF GONIOPLASTY

Acute angle closure is the term we apply to patients who often present with dramatic attacks of high pressure and severe symptoms. They usually have a uniformly narrow angle that, when it closes, closes entirely.

Subacute angle closure describes patients with intermittent symptoms of closure in whom only a portion of the angle closes. Chronic angle closure is applied to those in whom a portion of the angle gradually becomes narrow and then closes, with closure gradually progressing around the circumference of the angle without symptoms.

Selected patients with primary angle-closure glaucoma, particularly subacute and chronic cases, may be successfully treated with gonioplasty (Fig. 4). When the entire angle is uniformly narrow or closed, as in threatened or actual acute angle closure, other techniques such as laser or surgical iridectomy are more useful because pupillary block is a major factor and mere alteration of the anatomic configuration is not sufficient. However, if only a portion of the angle is narrow, alteration of the structural anatomic factor can be sufficient to widen and improve the angle in a clinically useful manner. In special cases of subacute and chronic angle closure, when a localized portion of the angle is narrow and in danger of apposition, alteration of the anatomic configuration of the iris rather than relief of the pupillary block is sufficient to prevent or retard localized closure. However, we do not recommend gonioplasty as a substitute for laser iridectomy if the element of pupillary block is the primary problem,

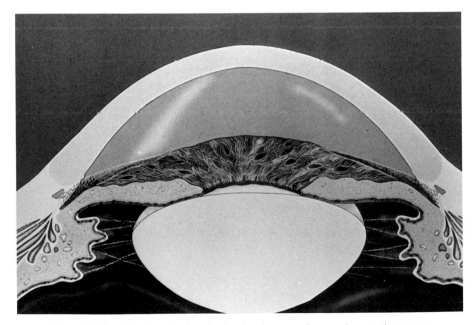

Figure 4. Gonioplasty effective for localized areas of narrowing or closure, as shown here in the central area of the iris, is appropriate for localized gonioplasty as depicted in Figure 1. The angle is open more peripherally and no gonioplasty therapy is needed for that portion of the iris. (*From Simmons RJ, Kimbrough RL, Belcher CD, et al.*[1])

as in primary acute angle-closure glaucoma. Rather, gonioplasty is useful in selected cases in which the angle configuration makes alteration of the mechanical factor an important and primary concern.

In both subacute and chronic primary angle-closure glaucoma, gonioplasty can be used in selected cases in which early synechiae are present. By applying laser energy to the peripheral iris at the base of the synechiae, early, partially adherent synechiae can be contracted enough to separate them from the trabecular meshwork. In early cases of angle-closure glaucoma in which residual peripheral anterior synechiae persist after a patent iridectomy has been made by surgery or by laser, gonioplasty can be applied to the base of the synechiae to contract the peripheral iris, partially separate early synechiae, and sometimes strip the synechiae completely.

Recently, a patient with an intraocular lens and pupillary block was referred to us for treatment. His referring ophthalmologist had correctly established the diagnosis of pupillary block with visible synechial closure of the angle. Although laser iridectomy was successful in relieving the block, the angle remained completely closed and could not be opened with Zeiss compression gonioscopy. Gonioplasty was performed and was successful in stripping the whole angle of synechiae. The eye has maintained an open angle with normal outflow demonstrated by tonography. This case demonstrates how early synechiae can be reversed by gonioplasty; not all cases with such extensive closure respond as well, particularly when synechiae are more long-standing and adherent, but in some cases, the end results can be gratifying.

Gonioplasty can be used if conventional surgery is refused or if the patient is too uncooperative for satisfactory laser iridectomy. In some of these patients, gonioplasty can be successfully employed to widen the angle, because it requires less precise application of the laser, and the lower energy settings employed produce less discomfort.

In early neovascular glaucoma,[7,8] gonioplasty can be used to separate early, weak peripheral anterior synechiae, in which the angle is starting to close and there are a few peaks in the periphery of the angle. In these eyes, laser burns are applied to the base of the synechiae on the iris side. If the synechiae are long-standing, gonioplasty may not be successful; however, if they are of recent onset and are weakly adherent, the synechiae can be reversed using this technique.

Nanophthalmos[2,9,10] (dwarf eye) presents a particularly challenging group of cases in which gonioplasty has been shown to be of significant value. Recognition and correct diagnosis of these cases are essential in applying the appropriate therapy. The most notable features of nanophthalmos are marked hypermetropia ranging between +8 to +16 diopters; small corneas; a small globe, with a short axial length of 15 to 17 mm; an ocular volume approximately two-thirds of normal; marked iris convexity; and shallow anterior chambers. While the globe has a short axial

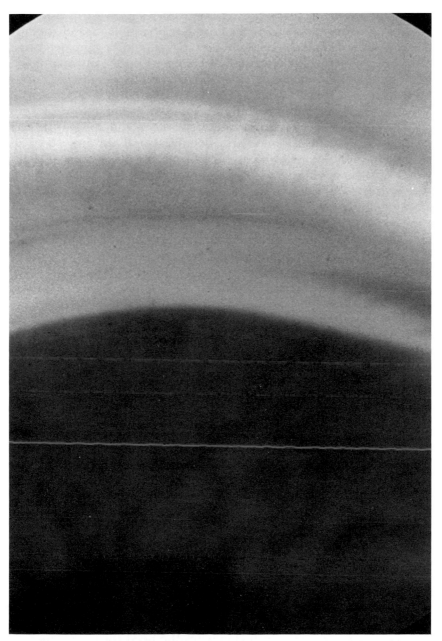

Figure 5. Prelaser gonioplasty, the angle is narrow or closed. No trabecular meshwork is visible. (*From Simmons RJ, Kimbrough RL, Belcher CD, et al.*[1])

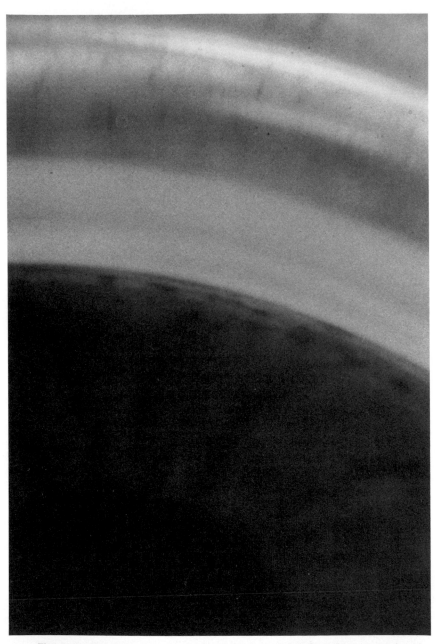

Figure 6. After laser gonioplasty, the angle is open and the trabecular meshwork is visible. Note laser spots on the peripheral iris. (*From Simmons RJ, Kimbrough RL, Belcher CD, et al.*[1])

Gonioplasty As an Adjunct to Laser Trabeculoplasty

In some instances, when laser trabeculoplasty is being performed, the trabecular meshwork is not adequately visible in some parts of the circumference of the angle because of peripheral iris convexity (Fig. 5). In these cases, localized gonioplasty burns applied to the iris in the narrow area will widen the angle sufficiently to provide an unobstructed view of the trabecular meshwork (Fig. 6). We have found that the addition of gonioplasty, to one and maybe two quadrants of the eye, has allowed increased visibility in those cases in which the angle is open by Koeppe gonioscopy, but the proper application of the laser beam is impossible because of the shape of the iris. Laser gonioplasty serves as a valuable adjunct in these cases to allow precise placement of laser burns for laser trabeculoplasty.

ACKNOWLEDGMENT

The authors would like to thank Sheila Attig for valuable help in preparing this manuscript.

REFERENCES

1. Simmons RJ, Kimbrough RL, Belcher CD, et al: Laser gonioplasty for special problems in angle closure glaucoma. In Transactions of the New Orleans Ophthalmological Society. St. Louis, CV Mosby, 1981, p 220
2. Kimbrough RL, Trempe CS, Brockhurst RJ, et al: Angle closure glaucoma in nanophthalmos. Arch Ophthalmol 88:572, 1979
3. Krasnov MM, Saprykin PI, Klatt A: Laser gonioplasty in glaucoma. Vestn Oftalmol 10:30, 1974
4. Hager H: Zur Lasermikrochirurgie bei Glaukom (Lasertrabekulopunktur [LTP], tangentiale Irisbasiskoagulation [TIK], Pupillenerweiterung und-verlagerung). Klin Monatsbl Augenheilkd 167:18, 1975
5. Perkins ES, Brown NAD: Laser treatment of glaucoma. In Amalric P (ed): International Glaucoma Symposium (Albi, France, 1974). Marseilles, Diffusion Generale de Librare, 1975
6. Worthen D: Unpublished data, 1979
7. Simmons RJ, Dueker DK, Kimbrough RL, et al: Goniophotocoagulation for neovascular glaucoma. Trans Am Acad Ophthalmol Otolaryngol 83:122, 1977
8. Simmons RJ, Dueker DK, Depperman SR: Role of anterior segment laser photocoagulation in prophylaxis and treatment of neovascular glaucoma. In Transactions of the New Orleans Ophthalmological Society. St. Louis, CV Mosby, 1981, p 391
9. Brockhurst RJ: Nanophthalmos with uveal effusion: A new clinical entity. Arch Ophthalmol 93:1289, 1975
10. Calhoun FP Jr: The management of glaucoma in nanophthalmos. Trans Am Ophthalmol Soc 73:97, 1975
11. Singh OS, Simmons RJ, Brockhurst RJ, et al: Nanophthalmos: A perspective on identification and therapy. Ophthalmology 89:1006, 1982.
12. Wand M, Grant WM, Simmons RJ, et al: Plateau iris syndrome. Trans Am Acad Ophthalmol Otolaryngol 83:122, 1977

CHAPTER 5

Laser Iridotomy

Historical Perspective

Alan L. Robin

Surgical iridectomies have been a safe and effective method of treating pupillary block glaucoma for over a century. Because the procedure is relatively simple, it is often the first intraocular surgical case performed by an ophthalmic resident. The concept of a broad-based iridectomy was first introduced by von Graefe in 1856[1] as therapy for glaucomas with very high intraocular pressure. It was not until 1920 that Curran[2] realized that this procedure worked best for cases in which the angle appeared narrow. In 1952, Chandler[3] introduced the currently used method of performing an iridectomy.

The procedure is relatively safe, but it is not without complications, although they are rare. These complications include incomplete iridectomies, wound leakage, flat anterior chambers, cataract formation, endophthalmitis, and malignant glaucoma. Another problem is that many patients who have been treated for an acute attack in one eye often are reluctant to have an iridectomy performed in their well-seeing fellow eye. To reduce these surgical complications, light energy has been harnessed to burn a hole in the iris without opening the eye.

The history of using light energy to produce holes in the iris actually predates the laser. In 1956, Meyer-Schwickerath[4] used xenon photocoagulation in attempts to burn a hole through the iris. However, problems with both corneal and lenticular opacification developed in these eyes because of the long delivery time. In 1964, Flocks and Zweng[5] attempted to use the ruby laser to produce iridotomies. Their work required repeated treatment for many incomplete iridotomies, and their methods

worked poorly in blue irides. Beckman,[6,7] using higher energy but a shorter time duration, was more consistently able to produce iridotomies. However, he also had less success with blue irides than with brown irides.

A great deal of credit must go to Zweng,[8] L'Esperance,[9] and Patz,[10] who from 1968 to 1972 reported their work of adapting a continuous-wave argon laser to a slit lamp. With this adaptation, there was low absorption of the laser energy by the ocular media (lens, cornea) and the burn produced by the laser was dependent on the presence of pigment and melanin granules. This pioneering work truly opened the door for the use of lasers in the treatment of both retinal-vascular diseases and glaucoma. Between 1970 and 1976, the first experimental work with the use of the continuous-wave argon laser in the production of iridotomies was published.[11-14] In 1978 and 1979,[15,16] short-term results reported that the argon laser was successful in producing iridotomies in the majority of eyes, and that these iridotomies relieved pupillary block.

One would expect then that this procedure would be widely adopted. However, there were some lingering doubts. Whether or not the whitish opacification of the lens, which sometimes occurred beneath the iridotomy following treatment, progressed to cause loss of vision secondary to cataract formation was a concern. We have found, however, that this whitish opacity represents a fibrous metaplasia in the area just beneath the anterior capsule of the lens, which remains localized for many years. There appears to be no other disruption to the remainder of the lens.

Another problem that was considered was whether the laser energy passing through the cornea to the iris could produce any damage to endothelial cells. Therefore, experiments were conducted on primates in which laser iridotomies were produced. The animals were sacrificed at varying time intervals following iridotomy, and their corneal endothelium was studied.[17] We found that there was no pleomorphism or loss of endothelial cells. What we did observe was deposition of both fibrous material and particulate debris on the endothelial surface. This was similar to the findings that one might expect in cases of uveitis.

Another question that occurred was whether or not the pigment released during the laser iridotomy procedure could obstruct the outflow mechanism, potentially causing a particulate glaucoma. Using primate research,[18] we discovered that pigment is originally found entrapped in the juxtacanalicular trabecular meshwork. This initial accumulation gradually dissipates over the course of a year. Pigment leaves the eye, both by bulk flow and by phagocytosis, through the endothelial cells in the trabecular meshwork. These endothelial cells possess the ability to detach themselves from the collagenous cores of the trabecular meshwork to become wandering phagocytes. At the end of 1 year, the trabecular meshwork appears normal by both light and transmission electron microscopy.

Primate research is informative, but the true long-term effects of laser iridotomies in humans is even more important. Quigley[19] and Pol-

TABLE 1. COMPARISON OF VISUAL ACUITY FOLLOWING EITHER LASER IRIDOTOMY OR SURGICAL IRIDECTOMY

Change in Visual Acuity	No. (%) of Eyes	
	Laser Iridotomy	*Surgical Iridectomy*
No change or improvement	52 (53)	47 (53)
Loss of 1 or 2 lines	33 (34)	17 (19)
Loss of 3 or 4 lines	9 (9)	9 (10)
Loss of 5 or 6 lines	0 (0)	4 (4)
Loss of > 6 lines	4 (4)	12 (14)
Total	98 (100)	89 (100)

(From Quigley HA: Ophthalmology 88:218, 1981.[19])

lack and this author[20] separately have conducted long-term follow-up studies. Our work dealt with 98 eyes on 54 consecutively treated patients with angle-closure glaucoma (mean follow-up, 53 months). All patients were followed up for at least 3 years, and none had significant visual loss. Fifty-three percent of the eyes either had the same or improved visual acuity as their preoperative levels; 87 percent were within two lines of their preoperative visual acuity. If this is compared with the results in eyes treated with surgical iridectomies (Table 1), we find no real significant difference. If we consider intraocular pressure control following iridotomy, we find that 50 percent of the eyes have their intraocular pressure controlled with just one medication. Only 11 percent of the eyes required surgical intervention, which compares favorably with other studies (Table 2) in which peripheral iridectomies were done surgically.

Because of the histologic and long-term follow-up work, we concluded that laser iridotomies are effective and safe. Complications related to intraocular surgery did not occur. No significant change in visual acuity or intraocular pressure control in eyes treated with laser iridotomy existed when compared to similar eyes treated with surgical iridotomies. Argon

TABLE 2. COMPARISON OF INTRAOCULAR PRESSURE (IOP) CONTROL AFTER LASER IRIDOTOMY AND SURGICAL IRIDECTOMY[19]

Methods of IOP Control	No. (%) of Eyes	
	Laser Iridotomy	*Surgical Iridectomy*
Iridotomy or iridectomy alone	49 (50)	209 (64)
Addition of one drug	24 (25)	48 (15)
Addition of multiple drugs and/or surgery	14 (14)	38 (11)
IOP uncontrolled	11 (11)	33 (10)
Total	98 (100)	328 (100)

(From Quigley HA: Ophthalmology 88:218, 1981.[19])

laser iridotomy, therefore, appears to be the preferred method of treating any form of pupillary block glaucoma.

REFERENCES

1. von Graefe A: Ueber die iridectomie bel glaucom und uber den glaucomatosen process. Arch Ophthalmol 3:456, 1857
2. Curran EJ: A new operation for glaucoma involving a new principle in the aetiology and treatment of chronic primary glaucoma. Arch Ophthalmol 49:131, 1920
3. Chandler PA: Narrow angle glaucoma. Arch Ophthalmol 47:695, 1952
4. Meyer-Schwickerath G: Erfahrungen mit der Lichtkoagulation der Netzhaut und der Iris. Doc Ophthalmol 10:91, 1956
5. Flocks M, Zweng C: Laser coagulation of ocular tissues. Arch Ophthalmol 72:604, 1964
6. Beckman H, Barraco R, Sugar IIS, et al: Laser iridectomies. Am J Ophthalmol 72:393, 1971
7. Beckman H, Sugar HS: Laser iridectomy therapy of glaucoma. Arch Ophthalmol 90:453, 1973
8. Zweng HC: Lasers in ophthalmology. In Wolbarscht ML (ed): Laser Application in Medicine and Biology. New York, Plenum Press, 1971, pp 239–254
9. L'Esperance FA Jr: An ophthalmic argon laser photocoagulation system: Design, construction, and laboratory investigations. Trans Am Ophthalmol Soc 66:827, 1968
10. Patz A: A guide to argon laser photocoagulation. Surv Ophthalmol 16:249, 1972
11. Khuri CH: Argon laser iridectomies. Am J Ophthalmol 76:490, 1973
12. L'Esperance FA Jr, James WA Jr: Argon laser photocoagulation of laser abnormalities. Trans Am Acad Ophthalmol Otolaryngol 79: 321, 1975
13. Abraham RK, Miller GL: Outpatient argon laser iridectomy for angle closure glaucoma: A two-year study. Trans Am Acad Ophthalmol Otolaryngol 79:529, 1975
14. Pollack IP, Patz A: Argon laser iridotomy: An experimental and clinical study. Ophthalmic Surg 7:22, 1976
15. Schwartz LW, Rodriques MM, Spaeth GL, et al: Argon laser iridotomy in the treatment of patients with primary angle closure or pupillary-block glaucoma: A clinicopathologic study. Ophthalmology 85:294, 1978
16. Podos SM, Kels BD, Moss AP, et al: Continuous wave argon laser iridectomy in angle-closure glaucoma. Am J Ophthalmol 88:836, 1979
17. Hirst LW, Robin AL, Sherman S, et al: Corneal endothelial changes after laser iridotomy and panretinal photocoagulation. Am J Ophthalmol 93:473, 1982
18. Robin AL, Pollack IP, Quigley HA, et al: Histologic studies of angle structures after laser iridotomy in primates. Arch Ophthalmol 100:1665, 1982
19. Quigley HA: Long-term follow-up of laser iridotomies. Ophthalmology 88:218, 1981
20. Robin AL, Pollack IP: Argon laser peripheral iridotomies in the treatment of primary angle closure glaucoma: Long-term follow-up. Arch Ophthalmol 100:919, 1982

Indications

Jacob T. Wilensky

The question of when to perform a laser iridotomy can be approached from two aspects: (1) when should a hole be made through the iris, and (2) how should that hole be created. Many articles and textbooks have already discussed the indications for iridectomy in much greater depth and detail, so this discussion will concentrate on the second question. In a few areas, however, where the availability of laser iridotomy has altered our indications for therapy, the first aspect of the question will be considered as well.

Laser iridotomy offers several clear advantages over surgical iridectomy. First, it is an outpatient procedure. Thus, in addition to saving the patient from the emotional trauma of a hospital admission, laser iridotomy means a much lower cost to the patient. Second, no surgical incision is necessary, so the risk of surgical complications such as endophthalmitis, flat anterior chamber, wound leakage, expulsive hemorrhage, or malignant glaucoma are eliminated. Third, the patient does not have to lie quietly on an operating table and there is no need for retrobulbar or general anesthesia. If the patient has a cough or a severe congestive heart condition, these will not seriously interfere with performing a laser iridotomy. Also, some of the long-term complications of surgical iridectomy may be reduced. Although localized focal lens opacities in the area of the laser iridotomy are frequently seen, it is our impression that late, visually significant, cataracts occur less frequently than after surgical iridectomy.

On the other hand, there are some definite disadvantages to laser iridotomy. It cannot be used on all eyes. The patient must be sufficiently awake and cooperative to sit at the laser and hold the head and eye steady. To create a laser iridotomy, the laser energy must be finely focused on the iris tissues. If corneal opacities, corneal edema, or irregularities of the corneal surface prevent the focusing of the laser beam sharply on the iris, then it will not be possible to create an iridotomy. There must be a formed anterior chamber. If there is not sufficient aqueous between the iris and cornea, the heat generated at the iris surface by the laser burns will burn the corneal endothelium as well (Fig. 1). In addition to damaging the endothelium, the opacities caused by these burns will interfere with creating the iridotomy.

A second set of disadvantages occurs with the significantly elevated IOP that is frequently seen following laser iridotomy. These transient pressure rises, which may be 20 mm Hg or more, potentially can be of much greater risk to an eye with advanced chronic angle-closure glaucoma than to an otherwise healthy eye that is having a prophylactic iridotomy. Moreover, there is a tendency for some laser iridotomies to close or heal over due to a proliferation of pigment epithelium at the edges of the iridotomy.

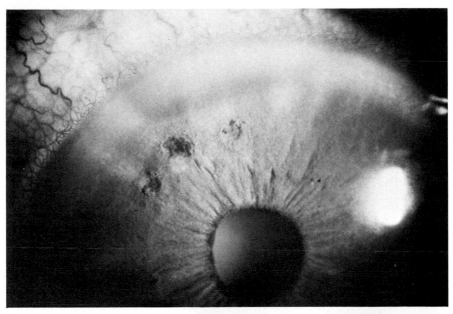

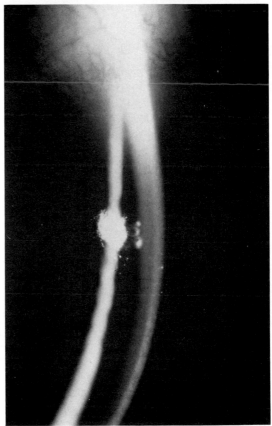

Figure 1. Damage to the corneal endothelium caused by the laser light while performing an iridotomy shown with (**A**) broad and (**B**) slit illumination.

The frequency with which this occurs varies with the treatment technique and the type of iris treated. We have found that approximately one-third of patients with light blue irides must be retreated during the first 4 to 6 weeks after the initial treatment because of this pigment epithelial proliferation. Late closures, however, are uncommon.

Still another problem is the inability to create a patent iridotomy on the first try. Creating laser iridotomies with an argon laser is an art that must be learned, at least partially by experience. The intensity, duration, and size of the laser burns must be varied from patient to patient, depending on the color of the iris, the health of the cornea, and the stage of the treatment (the parameters may be changed several times during a particular treatment session). For this reason the novice or occasional laser therapist may not be able to penetrate the iris completely during the first treatment session. In most situations this is of little consequence; the patient returns a week or two later and is retreated. There are, however, some situations in which it is imporant to have a patent iridotomy immediately, and in these cases the surgeon may opt for a surgical iridectomy if confidence in his or her ability as a laser therapist is lacking. There is, of course, the option of attempting an iridotomy with the laser and then proceeding to surgery if it fails.

Except for the contraindications listed above, we use laser iridotomy as our standard method of creating a hole in the iris as a primary procedure (versus a surgical procedure such as cataract extraction, corneal transplantation, or filtration surgery for which the iridectomy is secondary), even in acute angle-closure glaucoma attacks. In this last situation, we attempt to lower the IOP and break the attack by administrating hyperosmotic agents (oral glycerin, isosorbide, or intravenous mannitol), weak miotics (1 or 2 percent pilocarpine twice), and a carbonic anhydrase inhibitor. As the IOP drops, the cornea usually clears, and some anhydrous glycerin is instilled to further dehydrate the corneal epithelium. An Abraham iridotomy lens (Fig. 2) is placed on the eye, and treatment is commenced. Using this procedure, surgical iridectomy on all of the patients with acute angle-closure glaucoma treated during the past 2 years has not been necessary.

We stress again the fact that there is a marked difference between the response of different colored irides to argon laser energy. Very light-colored irides (light blue or green) contain little pigment to absorb the laser energy. Burns of longer duration and of higher power (0.1 second, 800 to 1000 mW) are required to create the burns. The dark-brown irides of black patients absorb the energy very well, but with burns of longer duration they have a tendency to char. The carbonized tissue forms a shiny surface that can reflect subsequent laser pulses rather than absorb the energy and convert it to heat. Thus, most success with dark irides is obtained by using multiple burns of short duration

Figure 2. Picture of an Abraham iridotomy lens. Note the high plus button bonded to the surface of a Goldmann fundus contact lens.

and low power (0.05 second, 500 mW). Light-brown or hazel irides are the easiest ones in which to create a laser iridotomy, and the inexperienced laser therapist would be well advised to begin with these eyes.

The most common indication for laser iridotomy is the prophylactic treatment of the fellow eye on a patient who has monocular angle-closure glaucoma. The second most common indication is for the treatment of chronic angle-closure glaucoma, for which the laser has really been an exceptional advantage. Traditionally, when dealing with a patient who has an angle that appears partially or totally closed, we have been faced with a dilemma: should an iridectomy be performed knowing that there may not be enough functioning trabecular meshwork to maintain the IOP at a normal level, or is a primary filtering procedure called for, knowing that in some patients a safer, simple iridectomy would suffice. With use of the laser, we can proceed with an iridotomy. If it works, then the patient has been saved an intraocular surgical procedure. If it fails, then the patient has to undergo only one, clearly indicated, operation. We have been very pleased with the number of chronic angle-closure patients, including some with an IOP in the 30s and 40s and advanced visual field loss, whose

IOP has been controlled following a laser iridotomy. Certainly some of these patients would have undergone filtering procedures unnecessarily without the availability of laser iridotomy.

Another fairly common indication for laser iridotomy is combined-mechanism glaucoma. By this we mean patients with mild to moderately elevated IOP who have been receiving glaucoma therapy for months to years and who on gonioscopy have very narrow angles, perhaps even with a clock hour or two of closure. When treating patients with this type of glaucoma, we are restricted in our medical therapy, fearing that the use of strong miotics and/or epinephrine may precipitate acute closure. By creating an iridotomy, this risk is eliminated and the use of all available medical therapy is allowed. We have been disappointed to find that the iridotomy by itself has little or no beneficial effect on control of IOP.

Although uncommon in this author's practice, laser iridotomy has been widely used to treat aphakic pupillary block glaucoma. For this condition, we find that it has a dual mode of action. In addition to creating a hole through the iris, the laser burns frequently cause a pull or tug on the iris at the pupillary margin that breaks adhesions between the iris and the vitreous face. When this happens, one can sometimes see the chamber deepen as the aqueous trapped in the posterior chamber streams forward through the pupil. Recently, there has been a definite increase in the incidence of acute aphakic pupillary block glaucoma associated with anterior chamber intraocular lens implants. Laser iridotomy can be used to treat many of these eyes successfully.

There is one area in which the role of laser iridotomy has not yet been defined. This is for uveitic angle-closure glaucoma with seclusion of the pupil and/or peripheral anterior synechiae. If keratic precipitates are too extensive or if there is too much protein or cellular reaction in the anterior chamber, it may not be possible to create a laser iridotomy. In most cases, however, a hole can be made (Fig. 3). As in the case of surgical iridectomies, many of these iridotomies may close over due to the continued inflammation. Because laser iridotomies are usually smaller and less peripheral than surgical iridectomies, we believe that they close quicker and more frequently (although they can be reopened quite easily). More importantly, we have yet to be convinced that laser iridotomies have a beneficial effect on the natural history of the disease, i.e., that they halt the development or progression of peripheral anterior synechiae. We will need larger numbers of patients and longer follow-up periods before guidelines for the use of laser iridotomy in uveitic glaucoma can be established.

In summary, laser iridotomy can be used in most situations that surgical iridectomy has been employed in the past. There are a few definite contraindications to laser iridotomy but these involve only a small percentage of patients with angle-closure glaucoma. Because of the reduced risks and complications, laser iridotomy has become the preferred tech-

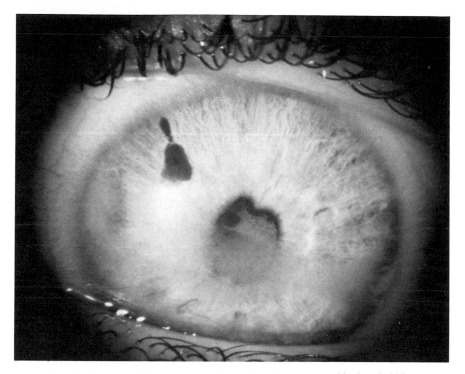

Figure 3. Laser iridotomy successfully performed in an eye with chronic iridocyclitis. Note the band keratopathy and bound down pupil.

nique of experienced laser therapists for creating iridotomies or iridectomies in most patients with glaucoma; moreover, there are certain situations in which it is almost mandatory, e.g., malignant glaucoma following surgical iridectomy in the other eye. In addition, because of the greater safety of the procedure, laser iridotomy is now being considered for certain borderline situations in which surgical iridectomy would be rejected.

Technique I

Irvin P. Pollack

It is very exciting to witness the changes that have occurred during the past 10 years in the treatment of glaucoma. The most recent of these, the use of the laser, has truly captured our imagination and has been tried in the treatment of virtually every form of glaucoma. Our experience with the laser began in 1973 when it was used to create iridotomies—first in

rabbits, then in monkeys, and finally in humans. Since that time, we have made therapeutic iridotomies in more than 1000 eyes.

I have mainly used the Coherent Radiation models #800 and #900 connected to a Zeiss slit lamp. The model #900 is equipped with a high-powered research laser that has a maximum power output of 5.5 W, whereas the model #800 had a maximum output of 3 W. We routinely use a modified Goldmann fundus contact lens (Abraham iridotomy lens) that has been coated to minimize reflection of the laser beam. This lens has a small planoconvex button lens, with a focal length of 15 mm bonded onto its anterior surface. The contact lens with its gonoscopic lens solution not only serves as a heat sink, but it also provides lid retraction and helps control small ocular movements. Its antireflective coating prevents light scatter and conserves laser energy for transmission. The planoconvex button converges the beam to a smaller spot and increases the energy density. It also provides additional magnification of the target site.[1]

Preoperatively, most glaucoma patients selected for laser iridotomies are already receiving miotics. If not, then I instill a drop of 1 percent pilocarpine 1 or 2 hours before the laser iridotomy is performed. If feasible, the patient is given a prescription for prednisolone 1 percent to be used four times a day, starting 1 day before treatment, and continued for 4 days after treatment. Because there is no guarantee that the iridotomy will remain patent, the patient is asked to continue all of the glaucoma medications throughout the postoperative period until we feel certain that the iridotomy is successful. In cases in which the intraocular pressure is considerably elevated prior to making the iridotomy, such as in chronic angle-closure glaucoma, the patient is provided with three 50-mg tablets of methazolamide, to be used the same evening after the laser treatment, and the next morning. In some cases the intraocular pressure rises to high levels within 24 hours of the laser treatment, and the carbonic anhydrase inhibitor will help lessen this increase.

A basic question is: What group of settings is best for making a laser iridotomy—to provide the least amount of laser power needed to produce the best penetration into the iris, with the least amount of thermal damage to the cornea and lens? We studied the effects of varying the laser power and pulse duration on the cornea and iris of cynomolgus monkeys that had been anesthetized with phencyclidine hydrochloride. The corneal burn was elevated for its density and width, and the iris lesion was judged for its width and depth. Both were graded on a scale of 1 to 4. The test sequence of instrument settings was as follows: increase the duration in increments of 0.01 to 0.2 second while increasing by steps the power from 1 to 5 W. We found that the best combination of laser settings occurred when we used 50- to 100-μ spot sizes for 0.2 second with power levels that were less than 2 W; however, these parameters required 200 or 300 applications of laser energy to produce the desired effect. With pulse times of 0.2 second, a satisfactory iridotomy could be achieved

with 30 to 80 applications. We have found that pulse times of longer than 0.2 second are often associated with burns of the corneal epithelium. Furthermore, the blink reflex occurs soon after 0.2 second, so that pulse times of 0.5 or 1 second are usually associated with more destruction to the iris stroma and little added benefit in achieving the iridotomy. For these reasons, we find it best to use a 50- to 100-µ spot size for 0.2 second, with a power of 700 to 1500 mW.

There are, however, occasions when the therapist will find it preferable to "chip away" with shorter pulses of 0.1 second, or to bore in with a longer pulse of 0.5 second. Flexibility of method and appropriate trials with these alternative pulses may assist in achieving an iridotomy and will reflect the skill and experience of the therapist.

In most cases one can simply select an iris site that is within a peripheral crypt (or in an otherwise desirable location), and proceed to treat. If the iris response is satisfactory and each successive application of laser energy deepens the pit into the iris stroma, then one simply continues to treat this site with as little destruction to the surrounding stroma as possible. If the iris response is poor after four or five applications, another site on the same or opposite side of the iris should be tried until a good response is obtained. One should never persist at an unresponsive spot, because another area may "melt" nicely before the laser beam. In some cases one can produce a "hump" or tenting of iris by applying two 400 mW applications along a radius of iris. A trough occurs between the two radial burns, while the iris below it becomes elevated to form a tent or hump. One can then treat the apex of the tent with 1 W of power for 0.2 second. Under ideal conditions, a deep pit into the iris will form at that point, and one can then proceed to treat it in the usual fashion. However, subsequent burns into the apex of the tent will flatten it, and a new hump will form below it.

In some persons with light blue irides, application of the laser burn will cause a thickening of iris at the site of the burn. If a second or third application at the same site continues to thicken the iris without producing a pit, then one should change the approach. Using a lower power (200 mW), a circle with a diameter of about 2 to 3 mm is made with six burns, leaving a thin, taut central region. This "drumhead" serves as a newly thinned region for laser treatment in the conventional fashion with settings of 0.2 second, 50-µ spot sizes, and 800 to 1000 mW.[2] Neither the drumhead method nor the iris tent, however, provides a magical answer to making a laser iridotomy. They simply allow an alternative approach for those few cases that do not respond satisfactorily to the usual treatment. Fortunately, in most cases one can simply pick a suitable site and treat until the iridotomy is completed.

The iridotomy can be placed anywhere peripheral to the pupillary sphincter or the point of pupillary block. However, it is preferable to make the iridotomy as far in the periphery as possible, beyond the con-

vexity of the lens where the iris is less likely to be in opposition to the lens capsule. The more peripheral the iridotomy, the less likely it is to produce a lenticular burn. At the same time, it is best to keep the burns inside the arcus senilis, when present, because the arcus will scatter the laser energy.

This author prefers to make the iridotomy in the superior iris in the area where it is covered by the upper eyelid. However, it is desirable to avoid the 12 o'clock position, where bubbles will remain in place and obscure the treatment site. We prefer the superonasal or superotemporal quadrant, where vaporization bubbles are easily dislodged.

It is imperative to be extremely careful to aim the laser beam away from the posterior pole at all times. When the superonasal quadrant is approached, it is best to aim the laser beam slightly nasally to assure that penetration of the iris by the laser beam will not cause harm to the posterior pole. Similarly, when treating the superotemporal quadrant, it is best to either change the patient's fixation point to a slightly temporal position or to aim the laser beam into the temporal periphery.

For many years we have been accustomed to making two iridotomies whenever a glaucoma patient is treated; this method is still used. This provides a safeguard in case one of the iridotomies should close. Closure of the iridotomy occurs by migration of pigment epithelium into the defect or because the defect becomes clogged with chunks of pigment epithelium from adjacent iris. We have shown in previous studies that iris closure usually occurs during the first week after treatment, but it can take place at any time within the first 5 or 6 weeks, after completing a laser iridotomy.[1] If the hole remains patent for 6 weeks it will remain patent thereafter, except in unusual circumstances such as during an episode of uveitis. Thus, it is important to follow up every patient carefully for at least 4 to 6 weeks after the laser iridotomy.

In summary, these helpful hints are important to remember:

1. Select instrument settings that are effective and yet minimize trauma to other tissues.
2. Use standard procedures, but maintain some flexibility of method.
3. Make the iridotomy in the iris periphery to avoid the lens, but remain more central than the arcus senilis.
4. Select an iris crypt or thinner area, when possible.
5. Do not persist at an unresponsive or resistant spot, but move to another area of iris.
6. Make the iridotomy in the superior iris, but avoid the 12 o'clock position.
7. Aim away from the posterior pole.
8. Use a fundus contact lens with gonioscopic solution.
9. If nystagmus is present or if the patient is unable to maintain fixation, do not hesitate to use a retrobulbar anesthetic.

10. Do not become unduly concerned about the persistence of a single stromal thread that bridges the iridotomy.

The ease with which a given laser iridotomy can be made depends partly on iris color and thickness, corneal tolerance and detumescence, anterior chamber depth, patient cooperation, and instrument quality. However, the rate of success also depends in large measure on the technician's skill and experience. This human factor of acquired skill and experience is of great importance.

REFERENCES

1. Pollack IP: Use of argon laser energy to produce iridotomies. Trans Am Ophthalmol Soc 77:674, 1980
2. Pollack IP, Patz A: Argon laser iridotomy: An experimental and clinical study. Ophthalmic Surg 7:22, 1976

Technique II
Hugh Beckman

It has long been my opinion that laser iridotomy is the treatment of choice for pupillary block glaucoma. As far as I am concerned, the only contraindication to it is the inability of the ophthalmologist to perform an iridotomy to cure the pupillary block being treated. Not all angle-closure glaucoma is pupillary block. We do not understand some of the causes of angle-closure glaucoma that is not pupillary block, but unless it is pupillary block, iridectomy or iridotomy will not relieve angle closure.

Basically, to perform a laser iridotomy, we must punch a large hole in the iris. Because the argon lasers that we use currently are marginal in power, a large degree of good technique and artistry is necessary to produce good iridotomies consistently. Figure 1 shows an iridotomy produced with use of a long pulsed ruby laser. It was created with a single pulse of 3.5J. The laser was set and aimed at the iris, and a hole was created in the pigmented eye. This can be accomplished every time, except in a blue iris. The iridotomy is about .75 to 1.0 mm in diameter, and it stays open.

The technique has a low complication rate. Sometimes, however, the aqueous overheats and produces an endothelial burn. Also, when the surrounding iris becomes overheated it too can cause a distortion of the pupil. Because of these complications, I decided to switch to argon lasers, which are readily available, although they may not be the ultimate instrument for this technique.

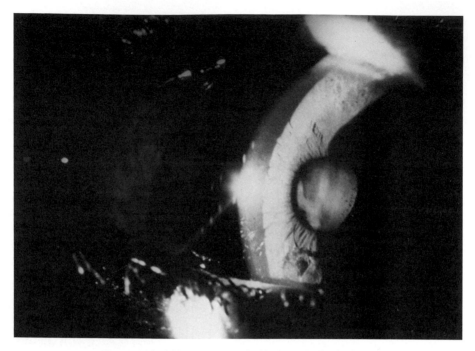

Figure 1. An iridotomy created with the pulsed ruby laser.

Most people call this technique an argon laser iridotomy. I always considered the holes made with the ruby laser to be iridectomies, because tissue is removed from the iris. With use of the argon, the procedure is called an iridotomy because the hole is small.

For the past 11 years I have successfully performed a laser iridotomy/iridectomy on every patient referred for that purpose. I find that the problem is not creating a hole, but keeping it open. Usually, holes do not stay open because they are too small. In such cases, the hole can be trimmed during retreatment. Clinically, trimming the holes is rarely a problem. Nonetheless, the objective should be to perform a reliable iridectomy of sufficient size every time.

Various techniques have been recommended for creating an iridotomy with the argon laser. Some laser therapists try to make a hump or a drumhead in the iris. I have tried both methods but no longer use them. The reason iris tightening techniques are needed is because some laser therapists apply energy to the iris at the edge of the crater rather than in the middle. If the edge is hit the iris tissue is sucked inward toward the center of the crater. When the next photon of light hits the edge, more fresh iris is pulled inside. To prevent this, iris mobility must be controlled as much as possible with miotic agents. Then as large a crater as possible

should be made. Treatment should be within this crater and the edges should be avoided.

I always place my iridectomies inferiorly to avoid the risk of inadvertent macular burns (Fig. 2). If treatment is done superiorly, vapor bubbles may get in the way, particularly in brown irides. The biggest aid in creating argon laser iridotomies has been the availability of the Abraham iridotomy lens. The lens develops a higher power density on the iris than on the cornea, which decreases corneal opacities and yields better visibility. A vital ingredient to a successful iridotomy is clear visibility. The iris really is a multilayered structure not a membrane, and therefore, it has depth.

In 1973 I reported that "present argon peak powers are not available to create iridectomies of the size that will remain reliably patent." I still believe that statement. Why do they not remain patent? The hole is too small. The posterior pigment epithelium folds together, or a late clump of pigment clogs the hole or a pigmented macrophage plugs the hole.

What happens to the laser beam as it enters the eye? It is absorbed in the cornea, in the superficial corneal and stromal tissue; it is also absorbed in the iris by the stroma, melanin, and connective tissue. It is important to understand that the argon wavelength is not absorbed by melanin only. It is actually absorbed by the stromal collagen, which is why iridotomies can be performed in blue irides with the argon laser. The pigment epithelium

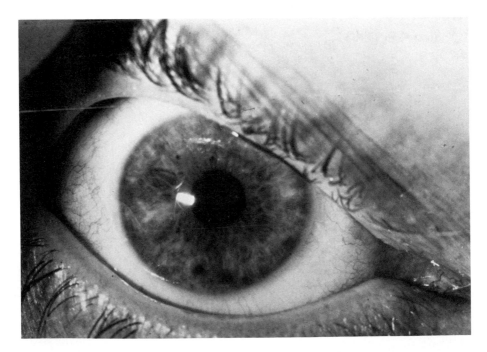

Figure 2. An iridotomy down near 6 o'clock created with an argon laser.

absorbs it beautifully, and one can see the pigment epithelium plume as the laser penetrates the iris. However, the tissues vary greatly from eye to eye and from place to place within the same iris.

How does one perform an argon laser iridotomy? First, the Abraham iridotomy lens must be used. Next, the area of the iris to be penetrated is chosen, and a test dose is given. It is not meant to be a penetrating dose; it merely demonstrates to the patient what the treatment is going to be like, so they will not flinch when you start to work. It gives you an idea of the patient's reaction and what effect the laser has on that particular hue of iris. You should always pick out a homogeneous area of iris. I do not like to work in a crypt; I find that they yield unreliable craters. I like to choose a flat piece of iris that is fairly uniform in color so that I can predict what will occur. The next step is to form a crater. For this step I generally use a 200-μ spot size, which achieves about an 80-μ burn with the Abraham lens. I will try a 100-μ spot if the 200-μ size does not work. I use about 600 mW of power in brown eyes and 1 W for blue eyes. The test dose is given at these settings for 0.1 second. For the actual crater formation, I use a 1-second exposure time for blue eyes and a 0.5-second exposure

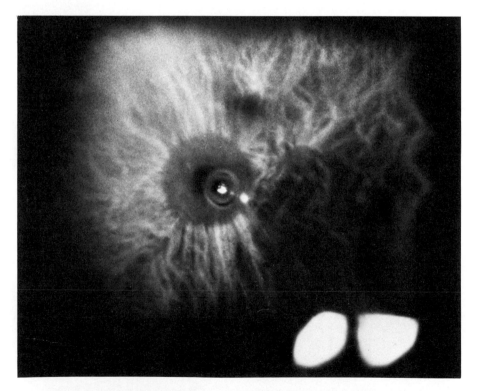

Figure 3. A small vapor bubble, generated while trying to create a laser iridotomy with the argon laser, obscures the treatment site.

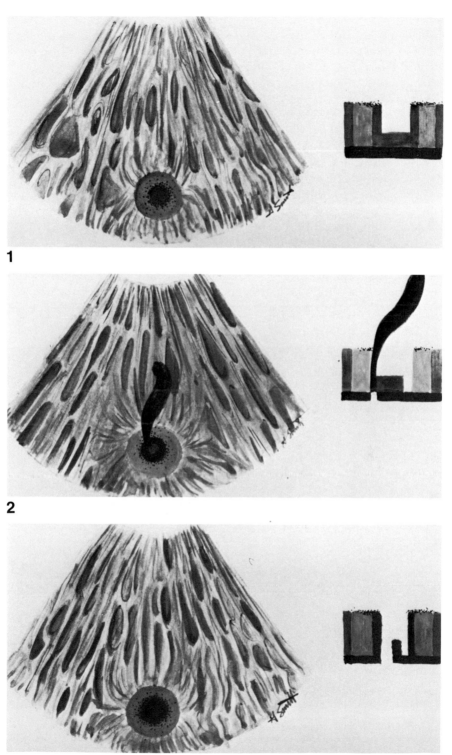

1

2

3

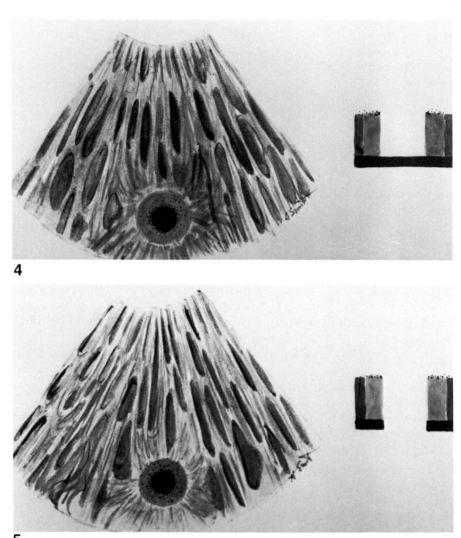

4

5 **Figure 4.** Stages in the creation of an argon laser iridotomy. (**1**) Creation of the
pit or crater. (**2**) Pigment plume as the pigment epithelium is partially penetrated.
(**3**) Complete penetration of the pigment epithelium but some epithelium remains
in place. (**4**) The iridotomy is occluded by a piece of pigment epithelium that fills
the hole that has been made. (**5**) The entire hole is open with clean edges.

time in brown eyes. After the crater or pit is created, then I work toward
penetration. I reduce the spot size to 50 μ, and use about 600 mW for
most brown eyes. I use the time selector to control duration of the crater
burn, but I can employ the foot pedal to control the duration of trimming
exposures.

The most important thing is to keep good visualization to see what
you are doing. If corneal edema develops, treatment will be difficult.

Also, you have to remove any bubbles that form (Fig. 3). If a bubble forms in the crater, I cut the duration to 0.1 second and flick the bubble out of the hole by hitting the bubble where it hits the iris. This will cause the bubble to pop off and float superiorly. Try to carve a cylinder down toward pigment epithelium without penetration. Studiously avoid the sides of the crater. You must watch for the pigment epithelium plume because it will herald penetration into the posterior chamber. You must be able to see the lens capsule when you are finished (Fig. 4). Make certain that you have eliminated any large pigment clumps. When I think that I have finished, I will wait a couple of minutes, because oftentimes a big chunk of pigment will float into the iridotomy site. This can then be cleaned out.

What are the problems? The biggest problem is adequate visualization. Blue eyes are easy to visualize, hazel eyes are second best, and brown eyes are hardest, because there is less contrast and you cannot differentiate pigment epithelium from stroma. Cooperativeness on the part of the patient is also a big factor. Trembling on the part of the patient can present a problem. Sometimes you have to wait while the patient relaxes. If the patient cannot hold the eye still, do not hesitate to administer a retrobulbar anesthetic; it will help tremendously.

If the anterior chamber is too shallow to work on, direct a small spot of energy at the pupillary margin. It will peak for a second, and the pupillary block can be broken right there. (Actually, if the eye has pupillary block glaucoma and you cannot produce a hole, you can break the block by notching the pupil.) One must also control the iris so that it is not sucked into the wound. The more pigment in the iris, the more heat. In addition, the shallower the anterior chamber, the more heat. Therefore, the darker the eye and the shallower the anterior chamber, the greater the need to move the site toward the pupil. Vapor bubbles cause a reflection of energy, which dances all over the eye. In general, in a brown eye the energy will dance over the anterior surface of the iris, which will cause more pucker. So whenever you see a bubble, flick it out.

A frequent problem with dark brown irides is carbonization of the crater. When a lot of melanin carbonization (char) occurs, further treatment is resisted. Because carbon does not contain water, it acts like a mirror. When you see charring, turn the power up and burn it off so that you can proceed with ease into the base of the crater.

To summarize my technique: (1) I do a test dose, which informs me of the kind of iris I am working with and it prepares the patient to hold still when I do the first long exposure shot. (2) I perform a trimming, in which I do my penetration doses. Generally, it takes me about 20 shots to penetrate after the initial shots. (3) I clean up the remaining pigment epithelium.

If one has selected the candidate appropriately, then one can

achieve success every time. One must, however, monitor the patient for the next 1 to 6 weeks to assure that the iridotomy is going to stay patent. These eyes must be followed up at appropriate intervals in case retreatment is necessary.

Results and Complications

Richard J. Simmons, Bradford J. Shingleton, and C. Davis Belcher, III

Laser iridectomy is rapidly replacing surgical iridectomy in the treatment of pupillary block glaucoma as the initial choice beyond medical therapy.[1-19] Because of its expanding role, all ophthalmologists need to have an understanding of the techniques, advantages, and disadvantages of laser iridectomy in creating iris colobomas. For this reason we have analyzed consecutive laser iridectomy cases from our group, which in addition to our own cases, include those of John V. Thomas, Stephen R. Deppermann, and Thomas M. Richardson. The technique, results, and complications of these cases were reviewed, and our recommended protocol derived from this experience is presented below. The terms "laser iridotomy" and "laser iridectomy" are both used widely and interchangeably to describe a coloboma of the iris created by laser energy. We will use the latter term, which seems to be gaining in usage.

In our first series (Series I), 102 consecutively treated eyes of 82 patients who permitted adequate follow-up were reviewed; the data from this series are presented here. A later series (Series II) consists of 63 eyes on which we performed laser iridectomies between October 15, 1981, and March 22, 1982. Series II is mentioned later in this chapter because experience derived from both Series I and II contributed to our current opinions on methods for performing laser iridectomy. In Series II, a higher percentage of cases was treated with our present recommended protocol. (The data from Series II will be presented at a later time after a sufficient follow-up period has been allowed.) These represent all patients brought to us for laser iridectomy from January 1, 1980, through October 15, 1981. The range of follow-up was from 2 ½ to 15 months (average follow-up, 4 months). There were 49 right eyes and 53 left eyes in the series from 51 women and 51 men. The average patient age was 65.8 years.

Diagnostic categories included:

1. Combined mechanism glaucoma: 38 eyes had open-angle glaucoma with a narrow angle component.
2. Narrow angles: 32 eyes had either positive darkroom test results,

positive mydriatic test findings, or angles that, by Koeppe gonioscopy, were closed or exceedingly narrow and considered highly likely to close.

3. Pupillary block with iris bombé: 13 patients had uveitis or rubeosis resulting in iris bombé with angle closure.
4. Aphakic pupillary block: 5 patients.
5. Primary acute angle-closure glaucoma: 4 eyes.
6. Central retinal vein occlusion with narrow angles: 3 eyes.
7. Imperforate surgical iridectomies: 3 eyes.
8. Nanophthalmos: 2 eyes.
9. Subluxated lens with intermittent pupillary block: 1 eye.
10. Pupillary block, status after scleral buckle: 1 eye. The treatment technique varied as experience was gained; however, the hump method or direct "chipping away" procedure represented the two major types utilized (the Coherent model 900 argon laser was used in this series). In the hump technique, a low-intensity burn of moderate duration and large spot size was placed at a convenient location, approximately one-half to two-thirds from the pupil to the limbus. This raised a hump or localized iris elevation above and below the burn. A full-thickness iridectomy was then made by placing a high intensity, moderate duration, and small spot size at the peak of one of the humps. The usual parameters for the hump technique utilized in our series were as follows:

- Stage 1: Production of iris hump. Spot size—500 μ, power—500 mW, time—0.5 second, applications—1. This is performed without utilizing the Abraham lens with convex button.
- Stage 2: Penetration. Spot size—50 μ, power—800 to 1000 mW, time—0.5 second, applications—1. This was performed utilizing the Abraham lens with convex button.
- Stage 3: Removal of residual pigment. Spot size—50 μ, power—250 to 1000 mW, time—0.05 to 0.2 second, applications—variable. This was performed utilizing the Abraham lens with convex button.

In the direct chipping away technique, no humping burns were made. Laser burns of high intensity, moderate duration, and small spot size were superimposed, one on top of the other, until a full-thickness opening was created. The usual parameters for the direct technique employed in our series utilizing the Abraham lens were as follows: spot size—50 μ, power—700 to 1500 mW, time—0.05 to 0.2 second, applications—variable.

With this baseline information, our results were as follows: 94 eyes were successfully treated and 8 eyes failed. Success was defined as the ability to make a laser iridectomy and to maintain its patency with mul-

tiple treatments, if necessary. Failure was defined as the inability to make a laser iridectomy or to maintain its patency.

Since the incidence of success and failure is important to our evaluation, it is necessary to pursue this breakdown further. We evaluated consecutive cases, that is, all cases that were brought to the laser with the intent of performing a laser iridectomy, between January 1, 1980, and October 31, 1981. This included two patients with corneal edema that precluded adequate beam focusing to perform an iridectomy and one patient who proved to be uncooperative for the procedure. At our current stage of knowledge, these three patients would not be considered for laser iridectomy at this time. We also had three patients with uveitis or rubeosis who failed. These patients represent a group with a much poorer overall prognosis for successful laser iridectomy. The remaining were two cooperative patients with clear media and no preexisting uveitis or rubeosis who failed. Both patients developed late closure of the laser iridectomy with subsequent angle closure and required surgical intervention. The first patient had a thermal sclerostomy and two choroidal taps, but decreased to light perception vision in one eye. The second patient had a subluxated lens with intermittent pupillary block and did well after an intracapsular cataract extraction and anterior vitrectomy.

We learned a very important lesson from the patient who required a thermal sclerostomy. She was from overseas and one of the earlier patients done in our series. Successful laser iridectomies were performed in both eyes for markedly narrow angles. She returned home and developed signs of angle closure, but did not see her physician. She did not return to our care until about 1 month later, when she was found to have an imperforate iridectomy, 360 degrees of synechial closure, and a pressure of 58 mm Hg. Because of the high incidence of early reclosure with laser iridectomies, but not with surgical iridectomies, it is clear that laser iridectomies can be performed only on those patients in whom careful and regular follow-up can be obtained.

If we consider only the eyes without unusual circumstances and exclude the unusual cases (two patients with marked corneal edema, one uncooperative patient, and the unique category of uveitis and/or rubeosis), we have 2 eyes of 86 that failed after laser iridectomy. This means that patent laser iridectomies were made and maintained in 84 of 86 patients, for a success rate of 97.5 percent.

An important concept to be appreciated, if laser iridectomy is to be accepted, is the frequent need for retreatment to widen or reopen previously made iridectomies. In 5 (5 percent) eyes (including the 3 eyes with corneal edema and the 1 uncooperative patient noted earlier), laser iridectomy was not possible on the initial attempt. A patent laser iridectomy was made in the initial laser session in 97 eyes. Fifty-two eyes (51 percent) required no further treatment to maintain a patent laser iridectomy. Forty-five eyes (44 percent) required one or more retreatment sessions to

widen or reopen a previously successful laser iridectomy. The majority of the patients requiring retreatment did not have fully closed iridectomies. Pupillary block remained relieved, but because of pigment accumulation or progressive narrowing it was thought best to widen the existing opening. In general, if the laser iridectomy showed 50 percent closure or more with pigment, it was reopened or widened with the laser.

The number of treatment sessions required to maintain the patent iridectomy in our overall series was as follows: 52 eyes required 1 treatment session; 30 eyes required 2 treatment sessions; 10 eyes required 3 treatment sessions; 1 eye required 4 treatment sessions; 1 eye required 6 treatment sessions; and 8 eyes did not succeed with laser iridectomy.

The direct chipping away technique was used for the retreatment sessions, with the following parameters: spot size—50 μ, power—200 to 1000 mW, time—0.05 to 0.2 second, applications—variable.

It is often stated that if closure occurs, it will take place within the first 6 weeks after treatment. This is generally true, but exceptions do occur. The average time from the initial laser iridectomy to the first retreatment session was 21.5 days (range—1 to 151 days). The average time from the first to the second treatment session was 40 days (range—1 to 1000 days).

The number of laser applications that were required to make an iridectomy varied with the treatment session. The average number of laser applications required to make a patent iridectomy at the initial treatment session was 37 (range—5 to 130). An average of 33 applications were required for the first retreatment session (range—4 to 106). An average of 24 applications were required for the second retreatment session (range—5 to 73). The limiting factor in all sessions was corneal clarity. There was no predictable or reproducible number of laser applications that resulted in corneal clouding. It is very common in laser iridectomies for a progressive accumulation of pigment to develop at the base of the opening. This may narrow or actually close the opening. This pigment accumulation is removed at the retreatment sessions. Because this pigment readily absorbs laser energy, easy reopening and widening of the laser iridectomy are achieved at retreatment sessions. Even large laser iridectomies may close, and it is dangerous to assume that they will not. We have seen such cases. Because late closure might be correlated with inflammatory response, all the patients in our series received topical steroids postoperatively. Postoperative dilation versus miosis did not influence the rate of reclosure.

The color of the iris has been known to effect the ease with which laser iridectomies can be performed. The relationship of iris color to the ease of treatment could be evaluated in 49 eyes in our series. Three color categories were selected: blue, light pigmented iris; hazel, moderate pigmentation; and brown, dark pigmentation. Sixteen blue eyes were included in this series of 49; in 8 of these patients only a single laser

treatment session was required to achieve and maintain a patent iridectomy. Eight patients required multiple sessions. An average number of 20 burns were required to perform the iridectomy. Nine hazel irides were evaluated: six iridectomies were performed in a single treatment session and three required multiple sessions. An average number of 45 laser applications were required to make the iridectomy in these patients. Twenty-four brown eyes were evaluated and only 7 iridectomies were done in a single session; 17 patients required multiple treatment sessions. An average of 50 laser applications were required in the brown irides to achieve a patent iridectomy. Of the three groups, brown eyes, therefore, required the highest number of laser applications and required retreatment most frequently to maintain patent iridectomies. Depending on whether there was a pigment clump on which to focus in blue eyes, laser iridectomies were either very easy or very difficult to make. Smaller openings tended to be made in blue irides, perhaps accounting for the higher rate of retreatment sessions when compared to hazel (moderately pigmented) irides.

Side effects associated with laser iridectomies were difficult to quantify objectively. A side effect for one patient may have been considered a normal finding for another patient or another surgeon. In addition, some findings were transient and not noted or mentioned by some patients or not believed to be complications by some surgeons. We compiled a list of anterior segment effects that may be encountered after laser iridectomies. Thirty-eight eyes in our series had the following side effects, which probably reflect an underestimation of those encountered: 22 eyes had transient epithelial and/or endothelial burns. The epithelial changes cleared in 1 to 2 days. An endothelial circinate ring opacity tended to clear in 4 to 6 weeks, although a remnant could usually be detected by retroillumination indefinitely. A focus of endothelial pigment persisted in some patients. No case of corneal decompensation was noted. Eleven patients had persistent corectopia, which involved a tenting of the pupil margin toward the area of the laser iridectomy. Transient corectopia of slight to moderate degree is frequent and tends to clear with time. One to 2+ pigmented cellular reaction, which is the rule after laser iridectomy, tends to clear in 2 to 3 weeks with topical steroid therapy. An occasional patient will have prolonged anterior chamber reaction for up to 2 months. Two eyes in our series developed a plastic iritis or fibrinoid reaction, which responded to intense topical steroid treatment. Posterior synechiae were noted in one eye. Focal anterior capsular or subcapsular opacities in the area of the laser iridectomy are probably frequent. These were well documented in three eyes in our series but were probably present in a much higher percentage of cases, since they were difficult to visualize well. There has been no evidence for progression of cataracts in these patients at this time, and this appeared to be of little consequence in other series; in our patients they often went unmentioned and unsought. Two eyes of one

patient had tension elevations of 15 and 17 mm Hg. This occurred the day after treatment, despite a deepening of the angle following the iridectomy. Both eyes responded to medical therapy. No retinal burns have been documented in our patients.

A review of the findings in the various diagnostic categories is as follows: 38 eyes had combined-mechanism glaucoma. These eyes had open-angle glaucoma with a narrow angle component. Successful iridectomies were achieved in 37 of 38 eyes (97 percent). With an average follow-up of 5 months, vision was noted to improve two lines or more in 1 patient, decrease two lines or more in 3 patients, and stay the same in 24 patients. No cataract progression was established, and vision was thought to have been unchanged by the iridectomy.

Thirty-two eyes had narrow angles. These eyes were not receiving medication and had no known associated open-angle glaucoma. These eyes either had positive darkroom test results or positive mydriatic test findings or were thought to have potentially closeable angles by gonioscopy. Successful iridectomies were achieved in 31 of 32 eyes (97 percent). The vision in these patients showed no apparent decrease over an average follow-up period of 5 months. Two patients were noted to have an improvement of vision of two lines or more, 1 patient had a vision decrease of two lines or more, and 24 patients maintained the same vision.

Thirteen patients had pupillary block with iris bombé secondary to uveitis and/or rubeosis. Successful iridectomies were achieved in 9 of these 13 eyes. The technique utilized in these patients was the direct chipping away. It was difficult to use the hump technique because the cornea was too close to the iris because of the iris bombé. The proximity of the iris to the endothelium of the cornea greatly increases the chance for corneal burns. The lower success rate noted in these patients was thought to be due to the more severe postoperative anterior chamber reaction that developed in these eyes.

Five patients with aphakic pupillary block were treated, two of whom had anterior chamber intraocular lenses. Successful iridectomies were achieved in four of these five patients. Once again the direct chipping away technique was utilized.

Four eyes had primary acute angle-closure glaucoma. Success was achieved in all four. In two of the eyes the attack was completely broken medically before laser iridotomy and the patient had normal intraocular tensions. In the other two eyes tensions remained high, with some component of pupillary block persisting. Three of the four eyes had mild corneal edema at the time of laser iridectomy. Therefore, it appears that mild corneal edema does not preclude successful iridectomy, however significant corneal haze may prevent it. Three patients had central retinal vein occlusions with narrow angles. Successful laser iridectomies were performed in all three, and the chamber was deepened sufficiently to permit goniophotocoagulation. Two eyes with nanophthalmos were suc-

cessfully treated. Three eyes with imperforate surgical iridectomies were successfully treated in one session. One patient with a subluxated lens and intermittent pupillary block was initially treated successfully but then developed late closure and required intracapsular cataract extraction with anterior vitrectomy. An additional patient with pupillary block following a scleral buckling operation was also successfully treated.

The effect of the hump versus the direct technique was evaluated. The hump technique was used in 66 eyes and the direct technique was used in 26. The remaining eyes were treated by a modification of either technique. Successful iridectomies were achieved in 65 of the 66 eyes treated by the hump technique. Success was achieved in 22 of the 26 eyes treated by the direct chipping away method. The lower success rate with the latter technique is probably attributed to the fact that more of the higher risk patients such as those with uveitis or rubeosis were treated by this technique.

On the basis of our series, the literature we reviewed, and our growing experience, laser iridectomy appears to be a safe and effective noninvasive procedure that should be possible in the majority of patients. The frequent need for retreatment must be understood both by the patient and by the physician and must be addressed prior to treatment. In addition, regular follow-up must be incorporated into the ongoing care for each patient.

As of March 1982, the members of our group have developed a currently recommended protocol. In our experience, it appears to be an efficient way to perform easy, atraumatic laser iridectomies with even more reliability and less complications than cited in the Series I, as tabulated earlier.

OUR RECOMMENDED TECHNIQUE

Intense miosis is produced with the administration of 4 percent pilocarpine, six times to the eye to be treated, at a minimum interval of one drop each 5 minutes for 30 minutes. If practical, a longer time between doses is even more desirable. Topical proparacaine is administered to the eye several times immediately before laser therapy. An Abraham lens is cleaned and filled with a clear goniofluid such as Methocel 4 percent (distributed by Haag-Streit). Care is taken that no bubbles are present in the goniofluid.

The patient is seated comfortably at the slit lamp, and the height of the slit lamp and the position of the patient's chin are adjusted for comfort. It is important that the patient's anterior body does not press on the slit lamp; otherwise, lack of control over the laser beam, inability to focus the laser beam, and motion of the laser beam will occur with the patient's breathing. By properly leaning the patient's upper torso toward the slit

lamp, one can avoid contact of the patient's body to the slit lamp itself. The patient is asked to close the jaw and keep the teeth together to facilitate fixation. The patient is asked to press the chin downward into the chin rest and the forehead against the brow rest of the slit lamp. A headstrap is placed behind the patient's head to help keep the head immobile. The patient is asked to hold the slit lamp table on either side so that further stability will be obtained.

Prior to initiating laser therapy, the reticles should be focused so that both oculars are appropriately focusing for optimal focus of the laser beam. The patient is asked to gaze upward, and the Abraham lens is inserted. The patient is then asked to look straight ahead. The slit lamp is focused and the light is aligned directly between the visual axes of the surgeon. The iris is then surveyed through the button of the Abraham lens. A site is selected in the upper temporal or upper nasal quadrant of the iris, in about the 10:30 or 1:30 o'clock meridian. An attempt is made to find a crypt where the iris appears to be thin. In a blue eye, an attempt is made to find a pigmented spot because the more darkly pigmented area will concentrate the laser energy and allow easy penetration.

The selected site should be approximately two-thirds of the way from the pupillary margin to the iris root and should be under clear cornea just inside the limbus. It need not be in the horizontal meridian or in the palpebral fissure. It is probably best to avoid the 11:00 to 1:00 o'clock regions directly above the pupil in case the patient should inadvertently move the eye and look into the laser beam. The laser iridectomy site for penetration may be relatively far to the periphery of the iris as long as it is inside the arcus and underlying clear cornea so that the laser beam passes to the iris through completely clear corneal tissue. An attempt is made to direct the laser beam toward the periphery, but if the beam is too oblique, the concentration of energy is not as great. A compromise has to be made between the desire to apply the laser beam relatively vertical to the iris, thereby concentrating energy and allowing the shortest passage through the iris for penetration, and the wish to avoid retinal burns. Because retinal burns have not been a problem in our cases, we believe that moderate or minimal slanting of the beam toward the periphery is satisfactory.

When the site for desired penetration is located, the first step of the iridectomy (step 1) is then undertaken.

Step 1 consists of applying *stretch burns,* which are placed in a square pattern around the site of the proposed penetration. These burns are of low intensity (200 mW for a blue iris and 100 or 50 mW for a brown iris). Very little energy is necessary because the applications are made through the button of the Abraham lens, which concentrates the energy. The intent is to contact the surface of the iris, as is done in gonioplasty (see chapter on Gonioplasty), but not to disrupt the surface and cause pigment dispersion or an explosion. These superficial burns stretch the iris between the corners of the square and do not distort the pupil. The applica-

tions are made with a spot size of 200 to 250 μ and a time setting of 0.2 second. Four applications are placed so that they are approximately 800 μ (four diameters of the 200-μ spot size) from the center of the square where penetration is desired. When the four applications have been made in the upper nasal quadrant, the lens is then turned to the upper temporal quadrant and a similar square or diamond is made with four applications in a similar manner around the site for desired penetration in that quadrant.

Step 2 consists of *penetration.* The site of desired penetration of the iris is located at the center of the square pattern, and the laser beam is set to 0.5 second, 0.5 W, and a 50-μ spot size. The beam is focused carefully at the site of desired penetration. The patient is warned not to move and that some discomfort or pain may be felt. The patient is cautioned against any movement of the body or the eye. Additional pressure is applied to the goniolens to press it more firmly against the eye, thereby inhibiting the opportunity for ocular movement. The beam should be focused as sharply as possible at the point of desired penetration.

The foot pedal is then depressed to allow laser beam application for the full 0.5-second duration. Immediately after application of the laser in this manner, one may see penetration through the iris. In some cases a bubble or debris is present at the iridectomy site. At this stage, one may proceed immediately to the other quadrant and apply a similar penetrating burn. This allows time for any debris or a bubble to disappear from the iridectomy in the other quadrant. One can then return to the original iridectomy site and survey it. If penetration is obvious, one goes on to step 3. If the iridectomy has not penetrated, a second, third, or fourth penetrating burn can be used. At the settings recommended, it is uncommon to obtain corneal burns.

If penetration cannot be achieved at these parameters with this technique, the laser settings can be altered. One can first use applications of greater intensity, that is 750 to 1000 mW but the same duration and spot size. If this is inadequate, and the cornea overlying the laser site remains clear, one can then increase the duration of the applications to 1 second. After several burns at this amount of energy and duration, the cornea frequently opacifies locally. If opacity of the overlying cornea is minimal and if near penetration has been achieved, it is possible to change the angle of incidence of the laser and still direct it at the base of the crater in the iris. After a few more applications, if no penetration is achieved, it is better to choose another site on the iris.

When penetration is not easy, one should avoid constantly reapplying laser energy to the eye and should consider alternate parameters or another site for penetration. As many laser surgeons have observed, one area on the iris will fail to allow penetration easily and yet an adjacent area may allow penetration with extreme ease.

We prefer to perform *two iridectomies,* because the chance of two

iridectomies closing simultaneously and producing unobserved angle closure is less than if only one iridectomy is present. Since the major danger in performing laser iridectomy is that closure of the site may be followed by unattended angle closure, this approach seems logical to us at the present time. During attempted penetration of the iris, it is helpful to think of the laser beam as a drill, since the laser beam, like a drill, should be applied to the deepest portion of the crater in the iris to gain the greatest likelihood of penetration. If the beam is directed to a different site each time it is applied, it will merely make another shallow crater, which does not add to the penetration achieved by previous burns.

Step 3 is that of *pigment removal* or *clean-up*. We use a 50-μ spot size, and occasionally a 100-μ spot size, with an energy level of 500 mW, and (as originally recommended to us by Dr. James Wise) a time of 0.05 second. The short duration allows one to disperse pigment from the base of the crater and to widen the iridectomy without producing contracture of collagen around the hole; otherwise, the hole may become smaller and tighter as the collagen contracts. For this stage, an attempt is made to disperse pigment granules in the base of the penetrated opening. If there are granules in a collarette around the inner aspect of the internal border of the hole, they can also be dispersed by directing the laser beam in a series of applications around the circumference of the hole. Frequently, it is necessary to disperse only pigment at the base of the hole so that the lens capsule can be clearly and easily visualized and so that no large pigment granules or clumps remain in the base of the iridectomy. After the first laser iridectomy site is cleaned up, the second laser iridectomy site can be attended to. Since pigment may migrate into the iridectomy site a few minutes after penetration has been achieved and even after the first clean-up, it may be necessary to perform additional clean-up to clear the sites.

Further clean-up or reopening can be performed 1 day to 4 weeks after the initial iridectomy. The settings used for the initial iridectomy should be employed. Penetration to reopen an iridectomy is usually easy as the pigment is commonly thin and readily absorbs the laser energy. To disperse the pigment from the entire crater, a long duration, such as used for initial penetration, is not necessary. If the iridectomy cannot be reopened, one can choose another site and repeat step 2. We examine our patients soon after the initial iridectomy is made so that reopening and clean-up can be achieved to avoid the danger of closure.

To help avoid reclosure, we medicate the patient with intensive topical steroids to decrease inflammation. We prescribe 1 percent prednisolone acetate, one drop every hour when the patient is awake for 48 hours after the iridectomy, and then four times a day for 1 week. While not every patient needs anti-inflammatory medication, by treating them all this way we have been able to avoid most inflammatory reactions. In addition, it is our custom to have the patients continue medical therapy, including miotics, after the laser iridectomy. If miotics were not part of

their ongoing therapy, we prescribe 1 percent pilocarpine four times a day temporarily to maintain the miotic state present at the end of the iridectomy. When we are confident that the iridectomy is well established and unlikely to close, this temporary miotic therapy is discontinued. If it is convenient for the patient, we often reopen or clean away pigment from the iridectomy as soon as a few hours to 1 day after the initial iridectomy. The patient is then followed up, if possible, for 6 to 8 weeks. After this, it is unlikely that closure will occur.

REFERENCES

1. Abraham RK, Miller GL: Outpatient argon laser iridectomy for angle closure glaucoma: A two-year study. Trans Am Acad Ophthalmol Otolaryngol 790:529, 1975
2. Abraham RK: Procedure for outpatient argon laser iridectomies for angle closure glaucoma. Int Ophthalmol Clin 16:1, 1976
3. Anderson DR, Forster RK, Lewis ML: Laser iridotomy for aphakic pupillary block. Arch Ophthalmol 93:343, 1975
4. Beckman H, Sugar HS: Laser iridectomy therapy of glaucoma. Arch Ophthalmol 90:453, 1973
5. Cooper RL, Constable IJ: Prevention of corneal burns during high energy laser iridotomy. Am J Ophthalmol 91(4):534, 1981
6. Fankhauser F, Roussel P, Steffen J, et al: Clinical studies on the efficiency of high power laser radiation upon some structures of anterior segment of the eye (Neodymium-YAG Q-switched). Int Ophthalmol Clin 3:129, 1981
7. Khuri CH: Argon laser iridectomies. Am J Ophthalmol 76:490, 1973
8. Mandelkorn RM, Mendelsohn AD, Olander KW, et al: Short exposure times in argon laser iridotomy. Ophthalmic Surg 12:805, 1981
9. Perkins ES: Laser iridotomy for secondary glaucoma. Trans Ophthalmol Soc UK 91:777, 1971
10. Perkins ES, Brown NAP: Iridotomy with a ruby laser. Br J Ophthalmol 57:487, 1973
11. Podos SM, Keles BD, Moss AP, et al: Continuous wave argon laser iridectomy in angle closure glaucoma. Am J Ophthalmol 88:836, 1979
12. Pollack IP: Use of argon laser energy to produce iridotomies. Trans Am Ophthalmol Soc 77:674, 1979
13. Pollack IP: Use of argon laser energy to produce iridotomies. Ophthalmic Surg 11:506, 1980
14. Pollack IP, Patz A: Argon laser iridotomy: An experimental and clinical study. Ophthalmic Surg 7:22, 1976
15. Quigley HA: Long-term follow up of laser iridotomy. Ophthalmology 88:218, 1981
16. Schwartz LW, Rodriques MM, Spaeth GL, et al: Argon laser iridotomy in the treatment of patients with primary angle closure glaucoma or pupillary block glaucoma: A clinicopathologic study. Ophthalmology 85:294, 1978
17. Snyder WB: Laser coagulation of the anterior segment. Arch Ophthalmol 77:93, 1967

18. Yassur Y, Melamed S, Cohen S, et al: Laser iridotomy in closed angle glaucoma. Arch Ophthalmol 97:1920, 1979
19. Zweng HC, Paris GL, Vassiliadis A, et al: Laser photocoagulation of the iris. Arch Ophthalmol 84:193, 1970

Comments

(*Editor's Note:* At the Symposium that gave rise to this book there were several question and answer sessions. I felt that some of the statements made about iridotomies provided information that might be of interest to many readers so I have added this "comment" section to the chapter.)

Dr. Pollack: Following both laser iridotomy and laser trabeculoplasty, a significant rise in intraocular pressure during the postoperative period can occur. We have studied groups of patients for 24 hours following iridotomy and trabeculoplasty. We measured their intraocular pressure every two hours on the day of treatment and again 24 hours later.

Following iridotomy there may be a great deal of debris and pigment dispersed into the aqueous humor along with a marked uveitis. This can be associated with a pressure rise of 10 to 20 mm Hg higher than the baseline value. Most of these cases have had a pretreatment intraocular pressure that was normal or near normal. Commonly, the acute attack has already been brought under control, or we are treating the fellow eye, or it is a case of chronic angle-closure glaucoma. Fortunately, most of our patients who undergo a laser iridotomy have a fairly healthy optic nerve and can withstand a pressure of 30 or 35 mm Hg for 24 hours fairly well. In our experience, many patients have a pressure elevation into the 30s and 40s.

We are especially concerned about any patient who has required more than the usual amount of laser treatment or whose baseline pressure is over 30 mm Hg. In these cases I prefer to take additional steps of caution. I prescribe three tablets of methazolamide (Neptazane) or acetazolamide (Diamox): one is taken immediately after treatment, the second at bedtime, and the third the following morning. If I am still concerned about the patient's pressure or if the patient is already taking a carbonic anhydrase inhibitor, then I will follow-up the patient carefully for 24 hours.

I was asked whether the fact that I routinely perform two iridotomies leads to an increased incidence of posttreatment pressure rise. A more appropriate question might be whether the frequency of pressure rise after laser iridotomy is as great now as it was 5 or 10 years ago. It is not. With experience one learns to make the iridotomy a little faster and easier and with less total energy. There is no question in my mind that the

frequency of pressure rise increases with the amount of energy delivered to the eye and the amount of trauma caused. However, I believe that I can make two or even three iridotomies in most eyes without excessive use of laser energy. The added benefit is if one of the iridotomies should close and other should remain open during the 4 to 6 weeks when closure occurs, then there is no need to retreat.

I have been asked whether aspirin or indomethacin blocks or decreases the pressure rise. We have not used aspirin to prevent the postoperative rise in intraocular pressure after laser iridotomy. We have studied topical cortiosteroids and topical flurbiprofen, a prostagladin synthetase inhibitor, and neither had a significant impact on lowering the incidence of postlaser rises in intraocular pressure.

Dr. Wilensky: We have been asked whether hemorrhage is a problem with laser iridotomy. With argon lasers it is not. Argon lasers work by burning tissue and coagulating blood vessels. If hemorrhage occurs, just place a few burns of a little longer duration over the bleeding site to take care of it. With the "cool" pulsed lasers such as the neodymium:YAG or Dr. Beckman's ruby laser, hemorrhage occurs fairly frequently, but usually is not of clinical significance.

Dr. Lieberman: We have been asked if the "cool" mode of the Britt argon laser offers any advantage when performing an iridotomy. Like most others here, I was trained on the Coherent lasers, but I have recently used the Britt Model 152. I have found it to be quite adequate and capable of performing all my laser needs for anterior and posterior work.

The cool mode has a dial with pulses up to 500 or so per second. The time interval (such as 0.2 or 0.5 second) can also be selected. It apparently provides a staccato-like delivery of energy, which theoretically generates less heat. Thus, it is very similar to techniques recently described for laser iridotomy using high levels of energy (such as 1200 mW) at short intervals (0.02 second). For iridotomies this cool mode often works well; it seems to spare the endothelium from clouding with lots of burns. By and large, though, I haven't found it markedly superior to the standard thermal delivery settings. I prefer to start with the cool mode and switch strands of iris that persist. I haven't used the cool mode for trabeculoplasties.

As an aside, I've used the Lasertek krypton laser a few times for iridotomies and would like to share my experiences with you. Keeping the power settings the same (1000 mW is the maximum level for krypton), I'd switch back and forth between the argon and krypton lasers. Both were equally effective to penetrate the iris—which was expected—since there isn't preferential absorption of the two wavelengths by blue or brown eyes. What impressed me was that, whereas the argon would cause slight endothelial burns and clouding, the krypton beam—at the same energy level and after the same number of burns—would not. I have no explanation for this.

CHAPTER 6

Treatment of Neovascular Glaucoma

Panretinal Photocoagulation

Lee M. Jampol

INTRODUCTION

Although rubeosis iridis has been reported with essential iris atrophy, iris neovascularization is only rarely associated with primary disease of the iris. It is almost always secondary to abnormalities elsewhere in the eye, particularly retinal vascular occlusive disease with capillary closure. The vessels of the iris appear to be the most susceptible in the eye to the development of neovascularization.

Considerable research has centered on the origin of new vessel growth in the eye including iris neovascularization. Some investigators believe that angiogenic factors are produced within the eye in response to ischemia, inflammation, tumors, and perhaps other stimuli. Michaelson, Ashton, Wise, and others have suggested that a *vasoproliferative factor* is responsible for vascular growth and that ischemic retina produces a diffusible substance that causes retinal, iris, or disc vessels to grow, presumably toward the highest concentration of the substance. When this factor reaches the anterior segment, rubeosis iridis ensues.

The nature of this "angiogenic factor of ischemia" remains uncertain. It has been proposed that lactic acid, tumor angiogenesis factor, growth factors (epidermal growth factor, fibroblast growth factor), or the prostaglandins are involved. Recently other theories have appeared to explain ocular neovascularization including rubeosis iridis. Wolbarsht and Landers have suggested that *venous dilation* "triggers" neovascularization, and they believe that tissue oxygen levels are important in this process. These

authors have hypothesized that hypoxia produces vasodilation, which in turn leads to neovascularization. Rubeosis iridis develops when the partial pressure of oxygen in the aqueous humor falls, causing iris vessel dilation and then neovascularization. The increased incidence of rubeosis iridis after vitrectomy and lensectomy is explained by the retina "stealing" anterior segment oxygen from the aqueous humor, which circulates posteriorly in the eye postoperatively. Sohan Hayreh has recently suggested that *vascular leakage* is an important predisposing factor to ocular neovascularization. He believes that diseases associated with increased vascular permeability result in neovascularization. All of these theories on the origin of rubeosis iridis are conjectural at present, and none so far explains all of the available data.

The majority of cases of rubeosis iridis are associated with ocular ischemic disease, usually of the retina. Diabetes mellitus is the most common cause, followed by ischemic central retinal vein occlusion and carotid artery disease. Rubeosis iridis is also seen in eyes with long-standing retinal detachment, especially aphakic eyes, particularly if a vitrectomy has been performed. Other causes include uveitis, ocular irradiation, retinoblastoma, melanoma, or ocular metastases. Most diabetic patients with rubeosis iridis have neovascularization of the retina and/or the disc. However, occasional diabetics with ischemic retinopathy without neovascularization may develop rubeosis iridis with no fundus neovascularization.

Central retinal vein occlusion is the second most common cause of rubeosis iridis. Hayreh has pointed out that most cases of central retinal vein occlusion can be classified as either ischemic (with extensive capillary closure) or nonischemic. In the ischemic variant, examination often demonstrates cotton-wool patches and areas of nonperfusion. Retinal arteriolar narrowing, sheathing, and closure are also noted. It is these patients who are at great risk of developing rubeosis iridis and rubeotic glaucoma.

CLINICAL EVALUATION OF RUBEOSIS IRIDIS

Slit-lamp biomicroscopy can be very helpful in the diagnosis of rubeosis iridis (Fig. 1). The first place to look for new vessel growth is the peripupillary area, but in a darkly pigmented iris early rubeosis can be difficult to detect. It also may be hard to distinguish normal iris vessels that are dilated from early neovascularization. Fluorescein angiography is much more sensitive in detecting rubeosis iridis (Fig. 2), but not everything in the iris that leaks is neovascular. Elderly patients and those with many other ocular diseases may show leakage of fluorescein from the iris without the presence of frank neovascularization. Visualization of iris vessels with all these techniques is more difficult in patients with darkly pigmented irides. Gonioscopy in patients with suspected rubeosis is important to determine if new vessels are visible in the anterior chamber angle and if synechial closure is present.

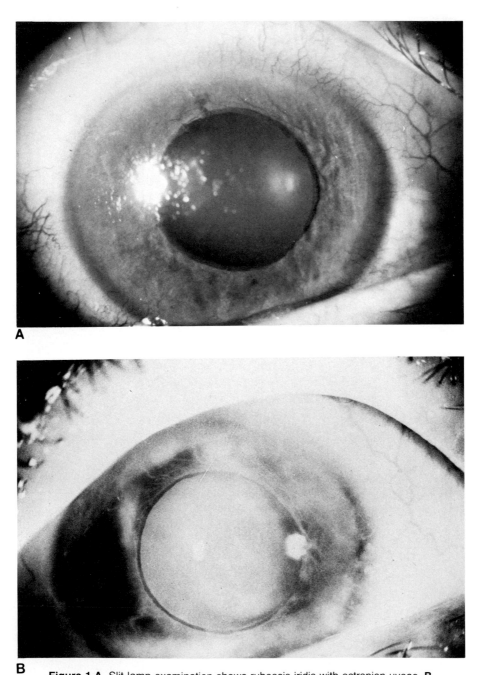

Figure 1.A. Slit-lamp examination shows rubeosis iridis with ectropion uveae. **B.** Extensive leakage is demonstrable with fluorescein angiography.

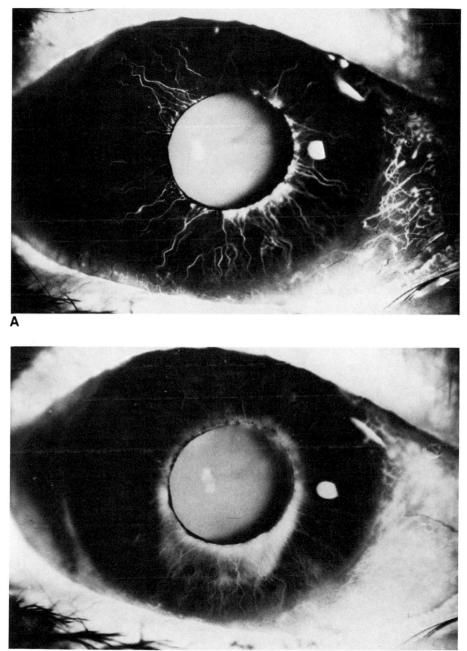

Figure 2.A. Early phase of fluorescein angiogram shows early peripupillary leakage. **B.** Late phase shows cloud of fluorescein extending into anterior chamber.

Wand and colleagues have classified rubeosis into four stages: *Stage 1* is the presence of just a few areas of neovascularization along the pupillary margin; with few exceptions, this is the first place that the vessels are seen. The stroma and angle are normal. *Stage 2* represents larger trunks of vessels in the stroma with pupillary changes, but again, gonioscopy reveals a normal angle. With *Stage 3*, neovascularization of the pupil and the iris stroma is present, and examination of the angle will show vessels bridging the trabecular meshwork, with the formation of small peripheral anterior synechiae. In *Stage 4*, this bridging of vessels has progressed to synechial closure of the angle. As will be discussed, it is well established that panretinal photocoagulation during the early stages of rubeosis iridis can prevent progression of the disesase. This has been proven in patients with diabetes mellitus, central retinal vein occlusion, and other ischemic fundus conditions. Whether this therapy will be helpful in patients with "inflammatory" rubeosis or rubeosis from other causes is uncertain.

Some patients who have rubeosis in the angle but no synechial closure may show elevated intraocular pressure. In these patients a thin membrane may obstruct the outflow, but it is not visible with gonioscopy. In most patients, however, glaucoma develops as synechial closure progresses. As the intraocular pressure rises, the cornea may become hazy. Ectropion uveae develops from scarring along the surface of the iris with eversion of the pigment epithelial margin. Posterior synechiae may also develop in these eyes. The rubeosis iridis may result in hyphema, but the major morbidity in these eyes is caused by the glaucoma, which is usually unresponsive to medical therapy.

PANRETINAL PHOTOCOAGULATION FOR RUBEOSIS IRIDIS

Data analysis from Boston has shown that eyes that have previously undergone photocoagulation for proliferative diabetic retinopathy have had a low incidence of developing subsequent rubeosis iridis. Even more important, however, is the demonstration that panretinal photocoagulation often has a therapeutic effect once rubeosis has appeared. Hunter Little and colleagues first reported this finding in 1976. A recent update of this group's data reported on panretinal photocoagulation in 32 eyes in 28 patients. These patients were divided into two groups. In 17 eyes there were less than 270 degrees of closure of the angle by peripheral anterior synechiae, and the intraocular pressure was less than 40 mm Hg. In 16 of these 17 eyes, the neovascularization disappeared and no further anterior synechiae developed. However, in 15 eyes with greater than 270 degrees of synechial closure or with intraocular pressure above 40 mm Hg no response occurred in terms of reduced pressure or regression of the rubeosis. Other investigators have confirmed regression of rubeosis iridis

with fundus photocoagulation in patients with diabetes, central retinal vein occlusion, and other conditions.

The mechanisms by which panretinal photocoagulation causes regression of the rubeosis remain uncertain. Proponents of an angiogenic factor of ischemia suggest that the panretinal photocoagulation may destroy a significant proportion of ischemic retina, thereby removing the source of the angiogenic factor. Another theory has suggested that the photocoagulation eliminates poorly perfused retinal vessels, thereby shifting blood flow to more adequately perfused areas. It has also been suggested that the photocoagulation may open channels for the transference of metabolic products (oxygen) through the pigment epithelium to the retina. The photocoagulation may also act by destroying the photoreceptors and pigment epithelium, thereby allowing more oxygen to reach the inner retinal layers. This hypothesis has been popularized by Wolbarsht and Landers. One can also suggest that photocoagulation may allow the entrance of inhibitory factors into the retina or the removal of angiogenic factors through the damaged blood-retinal barrier.

When photocoagulation is applied in patients with ischemic diabetic retinopathy or central retinal vein occlusion, the regression of the rubeosis iridis can be dramatic and may be seen within days of treatment. In general, synechiae that have previously formed are not affected. However, even if peripheral anterior synechiae have completely sealed the angle, panretinal photocoagulation may still play a role, as it may cause regression of the rubeosis and thus make subsequent filtering surgery or cyclocryotherapy somewhat safer.

INDICATIONS FOR PANRETINAL PHOTOCOAGULATION (PRP)

Not all patients with rubeosis iridis require photocoagulation. The indications for PRP will vary somewhat depending on the etiology of the rubeosis iridis. As has already been discussed, the two most common causes of rubeosis are diabetes mellitus and central retinal vein occlusion. The natural history of rubeosis iridis in diabetes mellitus is unpredictable. Patients may develop rubeosis that can be stationary for long periods of time or may even spontaneously regress. Therefore the mere presence of rubeosis is not an indication for PRP. Once vessels are seen bridging the angle from the iris root to the trabecular meshwork, however, PRP is indicated. If any of the angle has begun to close because of contraction of the fibrovascular membrane, the treatment must be initiated immediately. If the angle is already completely closed when the patient is first seen, PRP should still be performed if possible. This facilitates further medical or surgical management of the patient, particularly if glaucoma filtering surgery is being contemplated.

The management of rubeosis with central retinal vein occlusion is somewhat different. In the ischemic type of vein occlusion, the development of rubeosis iridis is common (about 50 percent of patients), rapid (often within 100 days of the occlusion), and almost invariably progresses to neovascular glaucoma. Therefore, when faced with a newly diagnosed patient with a central vein occlusion, the ophthalmologist's first step is to determine whether there is a significant element of retinal ischemia. Fluorescein angiography or angioscopy may be indicated, although retinal hemorrhages may make interpretation of the findings difficult. If significant ischemia is detected, prophylactic PRP is indicated. If ischemia is not found or the picture is equivocal, the patient can be followed up carefully every few weeks for evidence of early rubeosis. Iris angiography performed about 4 weeks after the occlusion may be of value. At the earliest sign of rubeosis, PRP should be performed. In the patient with a nonischemic central vein occlusion, rubeosis iridis is a very rare occurrence, so prophylactic PRP is not indicated. As with cases of diabetes, PRP should be performed in eyes in which angle closure is already present.

There is less information about the clinical course of patients with other causes of rubeosis iridis. In general, PRP should be reserved for eyes in which vessels are seen bridging the chamber angle or angle closure is already present. There is not yet sufficient experience to justify prophylactic PRP.

TECHNIQUES AND COMPLICATIONS OF PANRETINAL PHOTOCOAGULATION

Our experience with panretinal photocoagulation has been mostly with the blue-green argon laser. Most patients require only topical anesthesia, although some ophthalmologists prefer retrobulbar anesthesia. We utilize two types of photocoagulation lenses to apply the energy (Fig. 3). The standard coated Goldmann three-mirror lens has been utilized for many years for panretinal photocoagulation (PRP). One problem with this lens is that treatment is slow. Also, there is a zone between the area of posterior visualization and the most posterior mirror that is difficult to treat. One must make certain that the location of the macula is apparent so that photocoagulation is not applied in this area. The Rodenstock Panfundoscope is a contact lens that allows easy treatment of the posterior retina. The image is inverted and some experience is required to utilize the lens effectively. However, one gets a very large field of visualization that makes application of the posterior portion of the panretinal photocoagulation much easier than with the Goldmann lens.

The burn size produced is somewhat larger with the Rodenstock lens than with the standard Goldmann lens using the same laser spot size setting. For our photocoagulation we use the 500-μ spot size (less often, a

Figure 3. Goldmann-style three mirror lens (*left*) and a Panfundoscope (*right*) are used in performing panretinal photocoagulation.

200-μ size) whether a Goldmann lens or a Panfundoscope is utilized. Burns are placed throughout the peripheral fundus, beginning just inside the arcades and at the nasal margin of the disc (Fig. 4). The treatment is extended out to the equator, and sometimes to the ora serrata. We use 0.1- or 0.2-second duration and usually about 150 to 450 mW of power. The burns are randomly scattered and are separated by about one-half to one burn diameter. The average treatment consists of approximately 750 to 1500 spots, divided into two or three sessions, depending on the patient's cooperation. An advantage of not doing all the treatment in one session is that choroidal detachments are less common if less spots are applied. These choroidal detachments may result in shallowing of the anterior chamber and, in a few rare cases, in angle closure. As the panretinal photocoagulation is applied, areas of neovascularization elsewhere (NVE) in the retina are treated somewhat more intensely. Neovascularization of the disc is not treated directly. A response to treatment can often be seen within days (Fig. 5). If regression of the retinal, disc, and iris neovascularization is not achieved with 750 to 1500 spots, additional treatment can be applied; we have placed up to 3000 or more burns in some eyes.

Factors that may interfere with adequate therapy include corneal haze related to the elevated intraocular pressure, corneal opacities, uveitis, binding down of the pupil, cataract, and vitreous opacities including vitreous hemorrhage. In some eyes with a small pupil, the Panfundoscope

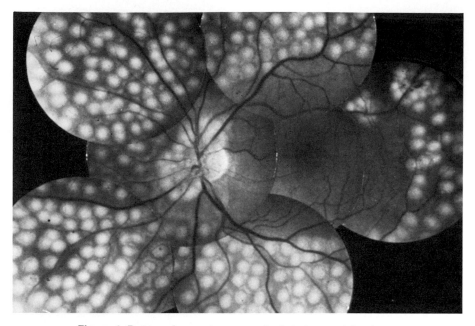

Figure 4. Pattern of argon laser panretinal photocoagulation burns.

allows treatment of the fundus when the Goldmann three-mirror lens cannot be utilized. However, the Panfundoscope usually requires clear media. Treatment may be more difficult in the presence of an intraocular lens or capsular remnants.

Complications of panretinal photocoagulation include the development of corneal epithelial or endothelial burns, lenticular burns (rare), uveitis, and a postoperative pressure rise. The corneal burns are transient, and the uveitis usually responds to topical therapy. Frequently the iris along the pupillary margin is slightly burned, but this is often of no significance. Loss of pupillary function and accommodation can occur, which may be very troublesome in young patients. With the application of many burns, choroidal detachment and shallowing of the anterior chamber can be produced (see above). Some patients complain of night blindness, and there may be a loss of far peripheral field, but this is usually asymptomatic. Other rare complications include the occurrence of macular pucker (epiretinal membrane).

If there are significant yellow lenticular changes, the red krypton laser may be more effective in creating retinal burns. The red light is less scattered than blue-green argon laser light. In addition, blood in the vitreous cavity tends to absorb the argon laser light, whereas the krypton laser may penetrate somewhat better. Thus in patients with significant cataract or vitreous hemorrhage, it may be possible to obtain burns in the

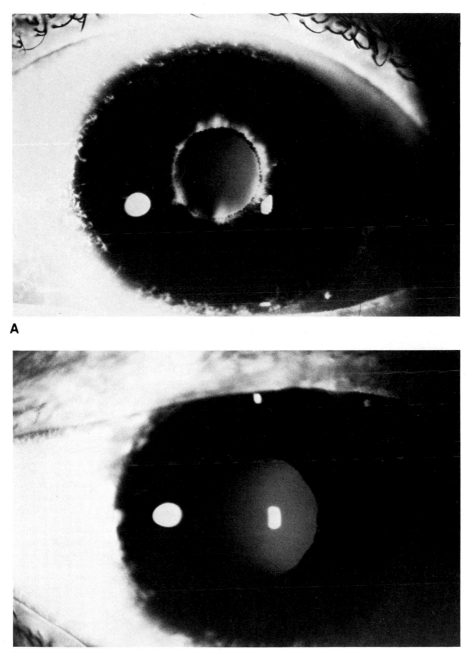

Figure 5.A. Leaking rubeosis iridis prior to photocoagulation. **B.** Disappearance of neovascularization after photocoagulation treatment.

fundus with the krypton laser but not with the blue-green argon laser. Moreover, in patients with many intraretinal hemorrhages, as from central retinal vein occlusion, the argon laser will frequently create superficial burns in the retina near the hemorrhage. However, the krypton laser may penetrate somewhat more deeply, thereby producing a therapeutic burn with less damage to the inner retina. If one waits for hemorrhages to clear before photocoagulating, rubeosis may have already developed. Preliminary evidence suggests that krypton laser photocoagulation is equally efficacious in causing regression of neovascularization of the retina, disc, and iris.

If the media are too hazy to allow any photocoagulation, it sometimes is still possible to do retinal cryopexy under visualization with an indirect ophthalmoscope. In this situation multiple retinal freezes can be done in an effort to destroy peripheral retina and cause regression of the neovascularization. Even if a conjunctival incision is not utilized, treatment can usually be extended back to the equator. If more extensive treatment is necessary, a conjunctival incision has to be performed. In eyes with rubeosis iridis and no visualization of the fundus, blind cryopexy can be applied in a heroic attempt to save the eye; however, this is often ineffective.

Retinal cryopexy can be combined with cyclocryotherapy for rubeotic glaucoma. In some patients, it is possible to do a partial panretinal photocoagulation, but cataract or other opacities block treatment of some parts of the fundus. In these eyes the photocoagulation can be supplemented with cryopexy. In eyes in which the rubeosis regresses but the pressure remains elevated because of angle closure, additional therapy for the rubeotic glaucoma is necessary. This may include cyclocryotherapy, filtering surgery, or placement of an artificial prosthesis for the exit of aqueous humor.

CONCLUSIONS

Panretinal photocoagulation is highly effective in causing regression of rubeosis iridis in a wide variety of ocular diseases. If it is applied early enough, rubeotic glaucoma may be avoided. The techniques and complications of panretinal photocoagulation are reviewed.

SELECTED REFERENCES

1. Henkind P: Ocular neovascularization. Am J Ophthalmol 85:287, 1978
2. Little HL, Rosenthal AR, Dellaporta A, et al: The effect of pan-retinal photocoagulation on rubeosis iridis. Am J Opthalmol 81: 804, 1976
3. Jacobson DR, Murphy RP, Rosenthal AR: The treatment of angle neovascularization with panretinal photocoagulation. Ophthalmology 86:1270, 1979

4. Gartner S, Henkind P: Neovascularization of the iris (rubeosis iridis). Surv Ophthalmol 22:291, 1978

5. Glaser BM, D'Amore PA, Michels RE, et al: The demonstration of angiogenic activity from ocular tissues. Ophthalmology 87:440, 1980

6. Wolbarsht ML, Landers MB III: The rationale of photocoagulation therapy for proliferative diabetic retinopathy: A review and a model. Ophthalmic Surg 11:235, 1980

7. Hayreh SS: Ocular neovascularization: An hypothesis. Int Ophthalmol 2:27, 1980

8. Weiter JJ, Zuckerman R: The influence of the photoreceptor—RPE complex on the inner retina. Ophthalmology 87:1133, 1980

9. May DR, Bergstrom TJ, Parmet AJ, et al: Treatment of neovascular glaucoma with transscleral panretinal cryopexy. Ophthalmology 87:1106, 1980

10. Wand M, Dueker DK, Aiello LM, et al: Effects of panretinal photocoagulation on rubeosis iridis, angle neovascularization, and neovascular glaucoma. Am J Ophthalmol 86:332, 1978

Goniophotocoagulation (Focal Angle Photocoagulation)

Richard J. Simmons, Omah S. Singh, and Stephen R. Deppermann

Goniophotocoagulation was coined in 1973[1] to describe the process by which argon laser therapy is used to destroy selectively progressive neovascular vessels in the anterior segment. The term *focal angle photocoagulation* has also been applied to this process. Because the area of recommended treatment has been extended from the angle and iris root to include serial photocoagulation of all anterior segment neovascular vessels, the term *pananterior segment photocoagulation* may now be more appropriate.[2] However, we are familiar with the original term of goniophotocoagulation and will continue to use it here.

The rationale for this modality of treatment is to destroy neovascular vessels directly, immediately, and repeatedly as they proliferate in the anterior segment, whether they appear in the anterior chamber angle, in the pupillary area, or on the iris stroma. It is important to initiate this therapy before the new vessels proliferate and result in neovascular angle closure, since closure of the angle is typically followed by severe intractable glaucoma, recurrent hyphema, chronic uveitis, and in severe cases, eventual loss of useful vision. After diagnosis of anterior segment neovascularization is made, several important considerations will influence the choice of treatment: (1) etiology; (2) rapidity of onset; (3) time lapse following diagnosis; (4) visible extent of neovascularization; (5) degree of angle closure; (6) intraocular pressure; and (7) previous ocular therapy (Fig. 1).

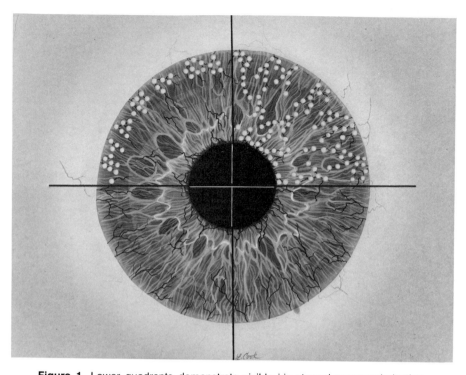

Figure 1. Lower quadrants demonstrate visible iris stromal neovascularization associated with angle neovascularization. (*Upper left*) Peripheral stromal vessels lasered in conjunction with treatment of angle. (*Upper right*) Stromal and pupillary vessels obliterated along with angle vessels at follow-up visits. (*From Simmons RJ, Dueker DK, Deppermann SR: Role of anterior segment laser photocoagulation in neovascular glaucoma. In Symposium on Glaucoma: Transactions of the New Orleans Academy of Ophthalmology. St. Louis, CV Mosby Co, 1981, p 395.*[4])

ETIOLOGY

The two most common conditions that result in progressive neovascularization of the anterior segment are diabetes mellitus and central retinal vein occlusion. In diabetes, anterior segment neovascularization is almost always associated with proliferative diabetic retinopathy. In progressive neovascularization from both diabetes and central retinal vein occlusion, areas of retinal capillary dropout are found on fluorescein angiography of the posterior segment. Less commonly progressive anterior segment neovascularization occurs in other vascular conditions resulting in chronic hypoxia such as carotid stenosis, carotid occlusion, and arterial occlusion.

Patients with central retinal vein occlusion tend to develop neovascularization within 90 days following the vascular accident, which makes this a crucial period for close observation.

Grant has pointed out that neovascularization develops in a recognizable progression and can often be detected in the early stages by very careful observation (Fig. 2). The earliest clinically visible changes are capillary buds and tufts at the pupillary margin; this alteration may sometimes involve only one quadrant initially. If iris angiography is available and can be performed at this time, fluorescein leakage confirms the abnormal permeability of these vessels.[1,3] After a variable interval of time this is followed by fragile neovascular vessels on the iris stroma in a random wandering pattern. The vessels in the angle characteristically begin at the iris base and extend linearly across the ciliary body band and scleral spur to the trabecular meshwork, where they arborize more extensively than can sometimes be visualized at this stage.

The neovascular vessels are accompanied by a membrane, which eventually contracts and produces closure of the angle. These vessels can also bleed, producing recurrent and sometimes massive hyphema into the anterior chamber with glaucoma.

Clinically, cases of anterior segment neovascularization may be thought of in two groups: a high risk group and a low risk group.

Figure 2. Early neovascular glaucoma. Gonioscopy discloses neovascular proliferation on iris and angle, with early synechiae. Most of angle remains open. (*From Simmons RJ, Dueker DK, Deppermann SR.*[4])

High Risk Groups

High risk cases are those in which there is a strong stimulus to the proliferation of new vessels in the anterior segment. Untreated, these cases characteristically show a rapid, massive onset of anterior segment neovascularization which, if unrecognized, results in neovascular glaucoma before effective measures can be instituted.

Group 1. Patients with advanced neovascularization before therapy have open angles but massive sheets of neovascular vessels in the angle at initial examination. Frequently, the vessels form a mat or layer of vessels so extensive that individual vessels cannot be recognized. Such cases are very advanced, have a very high likelihood of angle closure in spite of all measures, and should be treated urgently. A delay of a few days can lead to intractable angle closure.

Recommended is immediate treatment combined with simultaneous panretinal goniophotocoagulation combined with simultaneous panretinal photocoagulation and medical therapy, when indicated. The maximum amount of tolerated laser therapy is given initially, and the eyes are observed closely every day or two; repeated laser therapy is applied to all visible vessels in the angle at each visit. After therapy to the angle, the iris stroma and pupillary vessels are treated gradually in several sessions along the angle.

If the neovascular process appears to slow down and there is less proliferation of vessels, then the interval between visits can be gradually lengthened according to the response of the eye. In spite of heroic treatment, some of these eyes still progress to angle closure and neovascular glaucoma.

Group 2. Some cases show progression of anterior segment neovascularization in spite of panretinal photocoagulation.[4] These patients should be evaluated to ascertain that the maximum amount of panretinal photocoagulation has been used. Intensive anterior segment laser therapy is the only other prophylactic measure that is suitable, and must be applied promptly and intensively, as in Group 1.

Group 3. A population of patients with proliferative diabetic retinopathy have cataracts requiring extraction; these cases include a substantial number in young age groups. Patients with cataract and proliferative diabetic retinopathy should be carefully checked with gonioscopy before cataract removal. Often, the angle is wide open and there is no evidence of anterior segment neovascularization.

Following cataract removal, these patients should be closely monitored for early evidence of pupillary rubeosis. Gonioscopy should be performed as soon as possible after surgery. At the earliest indication of neovascular vessels in the angle, anterior segment laser therapy should be

initiated, followed by aggressive panretinal photocoagulation. In addition, the diabetic patient undergoing a cataract extraction should have the wound sutured tightly enough to tolerate the manipulations of gonioscopy and goniophotocoagulation, if needed. Also, retinal evaluation should be done soon after surgery for panretinal photocoagulation, when indicated. Any evidence of hyphema in such patients in the postoperative period should alert the ophthalmologist to the possibility that rapidly advancing neovascularization is present.

Group 4. Anterior segment goniophotocoagulation can be useful in preparation for glaucoma filtration surgery in patients with neovascular glaucoma. Such cases have a poor prognosis—the angles are usually closed and there is commonly iris and pupillary rubeosis, often associated with recurrent hyphema and inflammation. The success of filtration surgery in these neovascular glaucoma cases is poor in spite of the numerous variations and surgical techniques recommended in the literature.

Why use filtration surgery on such eyes? Cryotherapy is frequently the only other option to provide comfort. In our experience, cryotherapy has resulted in a marked decrease in vision in eyes with neovascular glaucoma. A recent analysis of 43 successive cases in our practice showed that, in nearly every neovascular glaucoma case with one or more applications of cryotherapy, the pressure could be reduced to near normal levels and the patient could be made comfortable. However, two-thirds of the patients had a major visual loss associated with the cryotherapy. We have, therefore, abandoned its use as an initial procedure in eyes with good visual activity. We currently choose filtration surgery after preparing the eye. We employ intensive medical therapy for several weeks to quiet the eye and reduce the intraocular pressure using steroids, antiglaucoma medications, and cycloplegics in some cases.

In addition, we obliterate all vessels in the anterior segment with panretinal segment photocoagulation. The vessels in the angle and on the iris are individually destroyed in a series of laser applications. Usually three to six separate sessions are directed at treating the anterior segment vessels. In our experience, many eyes have been quieted by this regimen and responded better to filtration surgery such as trabeculectomy or through-and-through sclerostomy procedures. The eyes frequently are more quiet and lack cells, flare, and injection after this approach.

Low Risk Cases

At the initial examination, a low risk case demonstrates a small number of vessels in the angle and anterior segment. When observed at regular intervals, initially every week or two, they show just slow progression.

In such cases, anterior segment goniophotocoagulation can be used as initial therapy. Control of the neovascular process can be achieved, anterior segment vessels can be destroyed, and posterior segment therapy

is unnecessary. It is our impression that the stimulus to neovascularization is minimal or declining. By obliterating the neovascular vessels in the anterior segment, the angle can be kept open and the anterior segment kept relatively free of vessels until the stimulus for neovascularization declines and/or subsides.

Cases with extensive capillary dropout in the posterior segment on fluorescein angiography have the strongest stimulus to neovascularization in the anterior segment. Cases of diabetes, vein occlusion, and possibly other disorders that do not show areas of capillary dropout have less chance of anterior segment neovascularization. With this in mind, we believe that posterior segment fluorescein angiography should be performed. Eyes with extensive areas of capillary dropout should be treated vigorously. Eyes with minimal posterior segment dropout should be observed carefully, but may be considered in the low risk group.

TECHNIQUE

Goniophotocoagulation is designed to destroy and obliterate neovascular vessels using the laser beam applied directly to the vessels (Fig. 3). The argon laser presently provides the most effective source of energy, using standard settings of 100- to 200-μ spot size, 0.2 second duration, and 100 mW to 1 W of power. If the spot size is too small, there is a high risk of perforating the vessel wall with bleeding rather than destroying the whole vessel. The eye is treated with a topical anesthetic such as proparacaine or cocaine drops, which provides sufficient anesthesia for anterior segment photocoagulation in the majority of cases. If the patient has a low pain threshold, a tender eye, or is extremely nervous, then retrobulbar anesthesia can be used.

The patient is placed at the laser slit lamp, and a three-mirror Goldmann lens is applied to the eye. The vessels are examined using high magnification, 25 × or 40 ×, since the smaller vessels are often difficult to see.

Laser burns are applied starting from the scleral spur and extending posteriorly to the iris root and peripheral iris along the course of each vessel. A test application is initially made using a low power of 100 to 200 mW, and the power is adjusted until visible blanching and constriction are noted in the treated area. If the vessel is not destroyed, then the treatment is ineffective. Once the effective parameters are obtained, then the vessel is treated along its course until it crosses the iris root onto the iris stroma. During the treatment, the power has to be varied often, since the response of the vessels is influenced by the degree of pigmentation in the surrounding tissue. If a small amount of oozing is noted from one of the treated vessels, then rapid laser applications are repeated in this area until

Figure 3. Goniophotocoagulation is applied to vessels starting at scleral spur and obliterating along vessels to peripheral iris. Laser to base of synechia can cause retraction. (*From Simmons RJ, Dueker DK, Deppermann SR.*[1])

the bleeding is stopped (Fig. 4). Precision and accuracy are important in this technique.

At the initial laser treatment, the aim is to destroy as many vessels in the angle as possible, and as much as the patient will tolerate. If stromal involvement is extensive, then an attempt should be made to treat the peripheral one-third of the iris surface. Pigmentation of the iris stroma will require lower power settings for effective vessel ablation. Also, patients find treatment to the iris more painful than to the angle. Care should be taken to avoid the trabecular meshwork; as little of this area should be destroyed as possible. If the iris is peaked with appositional or early synechial adherence, an attempt can be made to apply the laser beam to the synechiae to retract the iris from the angle wall (Fig. 5).

If at the initial examination the angle is completely closed, with or without the presence of glaucoma, then goniophotocoagulation is unlikely to be of significant value. The physician must then resort to medical therapy and, if necessary, to cryotherapy or filtration surgery. As described, goniophotocoagulation may be performed before filtration surgery in an attempt to provide an avascular bed.

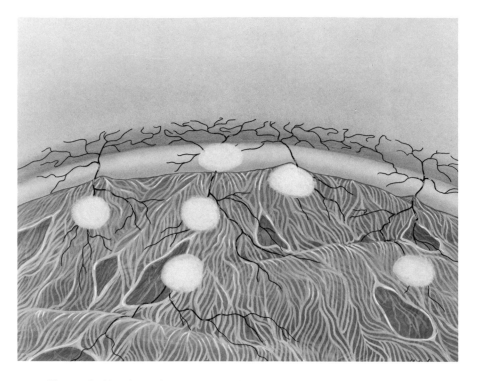

Figure 4. After laser therapy, areas of vessels are blanched where burns are applied. Old vessels will be retreated if indicated and new ones will be obliterated whenever possible. (*From Simmons RJ, Dueker DK, Deppermann SR.*[4])

RESULTS

The goals of goniophotocoagulation are (1) eliminate neovascular vessels in the treated portions of the anterior segment; (2) maintain an open angle and prevent further angle closure, where present; and (3) control intraocular pressure to 29 mm Hg or less with the combined use of medical therapy and laser treatment, where indicated.

Our results must be considered in the light that they are from a biased population sample, seen from 1973 through March 1981, in a private sector anterior segment-glaucoma referral practice. The cases were usually preselected by referring ophthalmologists. We analyzed the results of goniophotocoagulation in a total of 129 eyes of 107 patients. Of these, 103 eyes had diabetic retinopathy and 26 had central retinal vascular occlusion. The results continue to show a similar trend to our previously reported analysis.[5] Goniophotocoagulation was successful in 77 percent of the diabetic eyes. Using the same criteria as for the diabetic eyes, 62 percent of the central retinal vascular occlusion group showed a suc-

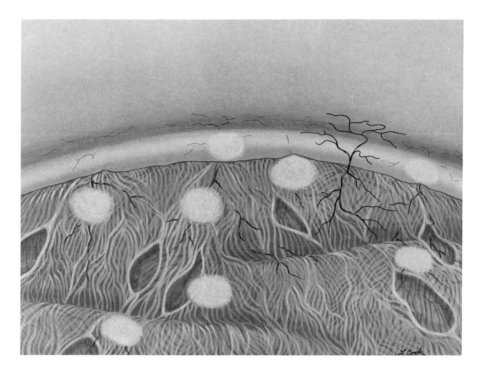

Figure 5. After laser therapy, angle and stroma are quite avascular. New vessels (*right side*) and remnants of old vessels require treatment. (*From Simmons RJ, Dueker DK, Deppermann SR.*[4])

cessful response. These results compare favorably with the experience reported by other observers in which 80 percent of diabetic eyes and 51 percent of eyes with central retinal vein occlusion did well. Using the indications for treatment defined earlier, goniophotocoagulation alone was used in approximately one-third of the eyes, and panretinal cryotherapy in conjunction with goniophotocoagulation in the remaining 4 percent. Absolute statistical conclusions are impossible from these results because of the preselected nature of our cases. Nevertheless, it is apparent that many patients with anterior segment neovascularization benefit from goniophotocoagulation.

The original group of patients reported on prior to the fall of 1979 were reevaluated as a separate subgroup. The follow-up period for this study was defined as the time interval between the first goniophotocoagulation treatment and the most recent gonioscopic examination, at which time the status of the treated angle was reevaluated. Of the original group of 88 eyes (73 patients), only 30 eyes were available for follow-up analysis: 23 were diabetic and 7 had central retinal vein occlusion. Of the 23 diabetic eyes, 21 showed a continuing successful result, with a follow-up

time of more than 13 months in 20 of these eyes. Eight of these 20 successful eyes had maintained success for more than 2 years. In the 7 eyes with central retinal vein occlusion, 6 had maintained a successful response to goniophotocoagulation for greater than 13 months.

These results suggest that, in a significant proportion of eyes inflicted with neovascularization, goniophotocoagulation has been successful in arresting the process for significant periods of time. In addition, patients with diabetic retinopathy and neovascular glaucoma often have other significant systemic factors (heart failure, renal failure, stroke) that contribute to a marked decrease in life expectancy. It should be considered a worthwhile achievement to have at least spared some of these individuals the pain and discomfort of neovascular glaucoma. In this series, 11 patients were referred for goniophotocoagulation of one eye following end-stage neovascular glaucoma of the other eye; in all 11 the neovascular process was stabilized with laser prophylaxis.

COMPLICATIONS

1. *Pain.* Topical anesthesia was adequate and effective in over 95 percent of the eyes treated. When retrobulbar anesthesia was indicated, it was administered with no complications.
2. *Transient iritis was more pronounced in the eyes in which extensive treatments were required.* These were successfully managed with the use of topical steroids for short periods of time.
3. *Microscopic hyphemas resulting from occasional bleeding of a treated vessel.* When bleeding occurs in a treated vessel, repeated laser applications should be applied until no further bleeding is noted from the vessel. No additional treatment is usually required for these microscopic hyphemas, and the eyes are usually quiet and clear after a few days.
4. *Gross hyphema.* Noted in three eyes, all cases with hyphemas gradually resolved with no deleterious effects.

DISCUSSION

Goniophotocoagulation is a useful and effective technique in the management of anterior segment neovascularization. It is a relatively safe procedure in which the complications are transient. Where rare cases of gross hyphemas of 3 to 4 mm were noted, these cleared with no damage to the eye.

Two important features to emphasize are a high index of suspicion for early diagnosis and careful case selection. The two well recognized groups in which this problem is known to occur frequently are patients with diabetes and those with central retinal vein occlusion. In the diabet-

ics, the high risk groups include patients with proliferative diabetic retinopathy of the posterior segment. Regular gonioscopy in these patients will often lead to early detection. The diabetic with cataract, when surgery is being considered, should be carefully monitored by gonioscopy before and after surgery.[5] In either of these two conditions, fluorescein angiography of the posterior segment should be obtained whenever possible and the patients showing large amounts of capillary dropout should be classified and treated as high risk cases for anterior segment neovascularization. Other subtle signs in these two groups can be the earliest detectable onset of pupillary rubeosis.

At first suspicion of neovascularization of the anterior segment, retinal evaluation should be performed. When treatment is considered for an affected eye, consideration must be given to laser therapy of both the anterior and posterior segments, initially with panretinal photocoagulation in conjunction with goniophotocoagulation. In the patient with cloudy media, in which the posterior pole cannot be adequately visualized for effective laser treatment, panretinal cryotherapy is a worthwhile alternative.

Once the diagnosis and initial treatment have been initiated, the eventual success is greatly influenced by the frequency of follow-up and treatment whenever neovascular vessels are noted. From the onset of laser treatment, it is very important to emphasize to the patient that one treatment does not constitute a cure, and that frequent follow-up visits and repeated treatments may be required before the neovascular process becomes controlled. In an eye with salvageable vision, when the angle closure is complete and the opportunity to maintain an open angle by laser therapy has been lost, the glaucoma should be managed medically, and laser treatment should be applied to the iris and the pupil to provide an avascular anterior segment for future filtration surgery.

Goniophotocoagulation is time consuming both for the physician and the patient. It should be used in conjunction, when appropriate, with other prophylactic treatment options for neovascular glaucoma, such as panretinal photocoagulation, medical treatment, cryotherapy, and filtration surgery. However, the potential for salvaging a substantial number of these eyes, for which treatment options are limited, makes goniophotocoagulation a worthwhile addition to the armamentarium against the previously hopeless entity of neovascular glaucoma.

(*Editor's Note:* In addition to techniques described in this chapter, there is one additional role for laser photocoagulation of new vessels on the iris. Some surgeons prefer to photocoagulate such vessels in the area where they will be performing an iridectomy during cataract or filtering surgery. Such treatment may reduce the risk of hemorrhaging or postoperative hyphema. Treatment parameters are similar to those given by Dr. Simmons in this chapter.)

REFERENCES

1. Simmons RJ, Dueker DK, Kimbrough RL, et al: Goniophotocoagulation for neovascular glaucoma. Trans Am Acad Ophthalmol Otolaryngol 83:80, 1977
2. Simmons RJ, Deppermann SR, Dueker DK: The role of goniophotocoagulation in neovascularization of the anterior chamber angle. Ophthalmology 87:79, 1980
3. Dueker DK: Neovascular glaucoma. In Chandler PA, Grant WM (eds): Glaucoma, ed. 2. Philadelphia, Lea & Febiger, 1979
4. Simmons RJ, Dueker DK, Deppermann SR: Symposium on Glaucoma: Transactions of the New Orleans Academy of Ophthalmology. St. Louis, CV Mosby Co, 1981, pp 391–402.
5. Simmons RJ, Boyd BF: Goniophotocoagulation for neovascular glaucoma: Personal interview. In Boyd BF (ed): Highlights of Ophthalmology: 20th Anniversary Edition, vol 15. Panama, Clinica Boyd, 1978–1979, pp 509–514

CHAPTER 7

Cyclotherapy

Transscleral Photocoagulation of the Ciliary Body

Hugh Beckman

I first reported on the technique of transscleral laser cyclocoagulation in 1972.[1] I am convinced of its superiority to cyclocryotherapy for the destruction of the ciliary body. While it has been clinically successful, it has been professionally frustrating, because no one else has had available a laser that could achieve these results. I am hopeful that with the rapid developments in laser technology (particularly the availability of the thermal mode neodymium:YAG laser) many other ophthalmologists will soon be capable of performing this treatment as well.

Transscleral laser cyclophotocoagulation is performed using a solid state (ruby or neodymium) pulsed laser that is connected to a Zeiss operating microscope (Fig. 1). A retrobulbar anesthetic of 1.5 percent nepivicaine with hyaluronidase is given. The lids are retracted with a speculum, and an opaque contact lens is placed over the cornea to prevent stray light from entering the pupil. The eye is marked into eight sectors, and 32 burns are placed 3.5 mm behind the limbus. Four treatment spots are placed in each sector (Fig. 2). The laser beam passes through the conjunctiva and sclera into the ciliary body, where it is absorbed by uveal melanin, and converted into heat. This heat causes the damage to the ciliary body (Fig. 3). There is considerable inflammation and reaction following the treatment (Fig. 4). The patient is treated with atropine drops for a few days and a mild corticosteroid preparation for about 2 or 3 weeks. In general, the intraocular pressure drops over a period of 2 weeks, reaches its nadir at about 2 weeks, and then tends to rebound as the eye whitens.

Following are the results from a series of cases that I have followed

up for more than 5 years. Some of these cases are from 1969 to 1970. I have now treated about 400 eyes but I have not personally followed up all of them, so the data are limited to 186 cases on which I have at least 6 months follow-up information. Most of these eyes had some form of intractable glaucoma that was difficult to categorize in many cases.

Table 1 summarizes the results in these 186 cases. The follow-up was from 6 to 108 months. My criterion for success in this series was an intraocular pressure greater than 8 mm Hg and less than 22 mm Hg. For destructive procedures, whether cyclocryotherapy, cyclocoagulation with a laser, or cyclodiathermy, many of the eyes being treated have hemorrhagic glaucoma. Hemorrhagic glaucoma has a high incidence of hypotony or phthisis bulbi, and it is necessary to consider the low as well as the high end of the pressure scale in talking about the success rate.

The success rate was 88 percent for the eight cases in the phakic chronic open angle glaucoma group. The one failure had too high an intraocular pressure (IOP). In the 38 eyes with aphakic chronic open-angle glaucoma, the success rate was 90 percent; 5 percent were failures because the IOP was too high and in 5 percent the IOP was too low. The 102 cases of neovascular glaucoma had a 55 percent success rate. The IOP was too high in 11 percent and too low in 35 percent. The 21 cases of secondary glaucoma had an 86 percent success rate; 5 percent failed because the pressure was too high, and 10 percent failed because it was too low. The 11 traumatic glaucoma cases had a 73 percent success rate. All failed cases had an IOP that remained too high. All six eyes with congenital glaucoma that I have treated have achieved successful control.

The review of cyclocryotherapy results compiled by DeRoth insinuated that brown eyes sometimes responded better to cyclocryotherapy than blue eyes. Therefore, I analyzed my results according to the color of the treated eye. The success rate was 75 percent in blue eyes, 73 percent in black, and 52 percent in brown. I checked whether the brown eyes had a higher prevalence of neovascular glaucoma, because most of the failures were in the neovascular group. This did not appear to be the case.

I would like to discuss several of these glaucoma entities in greater

TABLE 1. RESULTS IN 186 EYES TREATED WITH PULSED RUBY CYCLOTHERAPY (FOLLOW-UP 6 TO 108 MONTHS)

Type of Glaucoma	No. of Eyes	Success[a] (%)	Too High (%)	Too Low (%)
COAG[b] (phakic)	8	88	12	—
COAG[b] (aphakic)	38	90	5	5
Neovascular	102	55	11	35
Secondary	21	86	5	10
Traumatic	11	73	27	—
Congenital	6	100	—	—

[a]Success = IOP greater than 8 mm Hg but less than 22 mm Hg.
[b]COAG = Chronic open-angle glaucoma.

detail. Open-angle glaucoma in aphakia is a condition in which a variety of treatment methods has been tried: cyclodialysis, conventional filtration procedures, filtering combined with vitrectomy (as advocated by Herschler), partial thickness filtering (as advocated by Zimmerman), and cyclocryotherapy. None of these procedures has had a very high success rate. I actually divided the aphakic open-angle glaucoma patients into three groups: one group was treated with 6½ J of energy per burst, the second with 7 J, and the third group with 7½ J. (If nothing else, I want to impart that these are predetermined dosages. The laser is set up just like the argon laser. I apply 32 shots at 6½ J of energy per shot, circumlimbally at 3.5 mm. I am not spraying them with cold or galvanic current at a nondetermined rate. I know where the beam is and how much energy is in it. If nothing else, I have the superior destructive modality. It is a controllable, predictable, destructive modality that I can calibrate.)

The success rate in the aphakic open-angle glaucoma group was 90 percent; 5 percent had an IOP that was too low. I repeated the therapy only four times. Only one patient required postoperative medication and only one bad complication (phthisis) occurred in this group. The visual results were complicated, but basically only one patient lost vision as a result of having the procedure. Other patients may have lost vision owing to some complication of their underlying disease such as vitreous hemorrhage in a diabetic or uveitis in a uveitic patient. With the exception of one eye with plastic iritis and cataract formation, no case lost vision as a result of the cyclocoagulation done.

The burden has been to compare transscleral laser treatment with cyclocryotherapy. There are a large number of published results from cryotherapy, and I compared my results with the most favorable published results for cryotherapy. For aphakic open-angle glaucoma, the best published data are from Bellows. He reported a 92 percent success rate compared with 94 percent in my 7½ J series and 90 percent in my 6 J series, which means that our results are comparable. However, he repeated the treatment once in nine eyes and twice in one eye. I had to repeat my treatment only once. His findings were for 22 patients and mine were for 38. At the very least, a single ruby laser treatment is as effective as multiple cyclocryotherapies, with fewer patients requiring continued medication. Transscleral ciliary body destruction procedures are effective and relatively safe in the treatment of glaucoma in aphakia.

With ciliodestructive therapy of neovascular glaucoma the major problem is the incidence of phthisis. The problem is not reducing the pressure, but hypotony or phthisis. If the control of intraocular pressure and lack of pain is one's goal in rubeosis and hemorrhagic glaucoma, this procedure works fine, as does cyclocryotherapy. If the concern is vision, it is different. Vision is not easily retained once the patients have developed hemorrhagic glaucoma. The poor reputation of ciliodestructive procedures for neovascular glaucoma is not just due to the ciliodestructive

TABLE 2. COMPLICATION OF PULSED RUBY CYCLOTHERAPY

Complication	No. of Eyes
Phthisis	
Neovascular	
6.5 J burns	2
7.5 J burns	16
Aphakic COAG[a] 7.5 J burns	1
Secondary 7.5 J burns	2
Cystoid macular edema	2
Entopic phenomena	3
Subretinal effusion	1
Anterior segment necrosis	1
Plastic iritis	2
Cataract formation	2
Hyphema	
Neovascular	4
Other	1

[a]COAG = Chronic open-angle glaucoma.

procedures, but to the nature of the disease. The outflow is so embarrassed that slight changes in the rate of inflow can result in marked reduction of the IOP. The etiologic diseases are such that good visual results are uncommon. The success rates that have been reported with cyclocryotherapy in several different series include the following: Bigger Fiebel, 63 percent; Krupin, 34 percent; Bellows and Grant, 34 percent. With the ruby laser at 7½ J, it is 49 percent; at 6 J, it is 75 percent. The difference is less hypotony with 6 J. The visual results for all the series are poor. In my laser series, no patient that had vision lost vision because of the treatment. The 7½ J ruby laser cyclocoagulation is at least as effective as cyclocryotherapy in neovascular glaucoma, and the 6 J series seems even better. The complications (Table 2) were phthisis in 2 cases in the 6 J series and in 16 cases in the 7½ J series. One case had anterior chamber necrosis with cataract formation. There have been a few choroidal effusions. Interestingly, three patients have reported gold, floating balls in their field of vision years after the treatment.

Transscleral laser cyclotherapy has been known as a treatment for intractable glaucoma. I really use it for patients who are, in general, referred to me in desperate situations. Quite honestly, this therapy may be used in more general cases in the future, especially with the use of the neodymium or dye laser.

REFERENCE

1. Beckman H, Kinoshita A, Rota AN, et al: Transscleral ruby laser irradiation of ciliary body in the treatment of intractable glaucoma. Trans Am Acad Ophthalmol Otolaryngol 76:423, 1972

Transpupillary Argon Laser Photocoagulation of Ciliary Processes

Edward Goldman and Jacob T. Wilensky

Several ciliodestructive techniques have been developed to control intra-ocular pressure (IOP) when conventional medical and surgical management has failed. With cyclodiathermy, success is variable and the incidence of postoperative complications approaches the rate of success. Similar complications and failures occur with the use of cyclocryotherapy, in which the appropriate amount of treatment is narrowly bordered by hypotony resulting from overtreatment, or IOP returns to its pretreatment level because of procedure failure.

The development of the laser led to new investigations. In 1971, Lee and Pomerantzeff[1] reported results of rabbit eyes treated with transpupillary argon laser photocoagulation of the ciliary processes. After two or three clock hours of ciliary processes were treated, close to 90 percent of the eyes showed a significant reduction of IOP for up to 12 months.

The first report of clinical application appeared in 1973.[2] Four eyes were treated in that study, and after a follow-up of only 10 weeks the authors abandoned the procedure as a failure. In 1976, another report indicated treatment failure in six of seven treated eyes.[3] In 1979, Lee[4] described the results of 14 aphakic eyes with severe glaucoma. Ten of the 14 eyes benefited from the procedure; the average follow-up period was 2½ years.

These three reports indicate widely variable success rates. It is necessary, therefore, to examine each report closely because the procedure was not performed in the same manner. The end point of photocoagulation in the studies done by Zimmerman et al[2] and Merritt[3] was whitening of the ciliary processes, while the end point of photocoagulation for Lee[4] was a concave burn with pigment dispersion or gas bubble formation. The energy used to achieve the latter end point was between four and seven times that used in the initial two studies. In addition, Lee performed multiple treatment sessions to achieve the desired therapeutic result.

We treated a small series of patients with transpupillary laser cyclotherapy. We used 100-μ laser burns for 0.1 second at 1000 mW of power on five patients with medically uncontrollable glaucoma (Fig. 1). Each ciliary process was treated until there was pigment dispersion or gas bubble formation. Five patients were followed up for a period of 8 to 17 months (Table 1). Most of the patients required more than one treatment.

RESULTS

Patient 1 had an intracapsular cataract extraction. Postoperatively, the course was complicated by a flat anterior chamber and, later, elevated

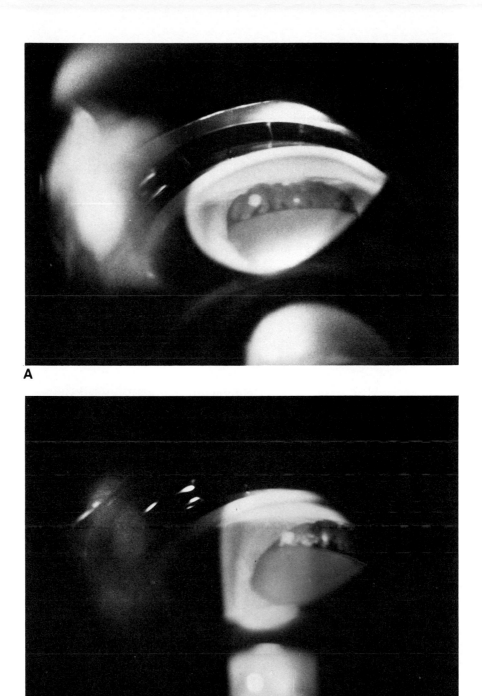

A

B

Figure 1.A. Argon laser light focused on the ciliary processes in a patient with a peripheral iridectomy. No processes have been photocoagulated yet. **B.** The processes on the left have now been photocoagulated and have been blanched. The white color of these processes is not due to the laser light being shown on them, as is the case with the third process, but the result of the treatment.

TABLE 1.

Patient No.	Ocular History	Follow-up Period After Treatment (mo)
1	Aphakic, previous cyclocryo-therapy, filter	13
2	Diabetic, aphakic	15
3	Angle-closure, rubeosis iridis, diabetic, aphakic	8
4	Diabetic, aphakic, previous cyclocryotherapy, closed angle	12
5	Diabetic, angle recession, previous filter, cyclocryotherapy	17

IOP. One month postoperatively she underwent cyclocryotherapy for a pressure of 44 mm Hg that could not be lowered with medication. The pressure remained high after cyclocryotherapy and the patient had a trabeculectomy 3 months after cataract surgery. For approximately 2½ years the pressure was controlled medically, but then the IOP again rose to 43 mm Hg. Ten ciliary processes were treated with the argon laser. The postoperative course was marked with variable IOP readings (Fig. 2). A total of three treatments were attempted before cyclocryotherapy was again tried 13 months later. During the entire treatment period the patient was receiving phospholine iodide and/or timolol, as needed, to help keep the IOP under control.

Patient 2 was a 64-year-old diabetic woman who underwent cataract extraction in January 1980. One year postoperatively she was found to have marked rubeosis iridis with a closed angle and an IOP of 67 mm Hg that could not be lowered with timolol and propine. The patient underwent laser treatment to approximately 20 ciliary processes on two occasions. Postoperatively (Fig. 3) the patient's IOP was controlled with timolol and propine.

Patient 3 was a 62-year-old diabetic man. Eight months after cataract extraction he developed marked rubeosis iridis with a closed angle and an IOP of 58 mm Hg. The IOP could not be controlled with timolol, and the patient underwent laser treatment to 14 ciliary processes. His postoperative course is shown in Figure 4. When last seen his pressure was 34 mm Hg with use of timolol and acetazolamide.

Patient 4 was a 59-year-old diabetic woman with a positive serologic test for syphilis who underwent cataract surgery in 1972 with postoperative complications of recurrent hyphema and a flat anterior chamber. Subsequent elevations of IOP were unresponsive to miotics and were treated with cyclocryotherapy. The IOP fluctuated between 14 and 60 mm Hg with medical therapy. In February 1981 she underwent laser

treatment to the ciliary processes because her IOP was 36 mm Hg. Within 1 week the IOP was elevated again and the same processes were retreated. After therapy the IOP has fluctuated widely (Fig. 5). During this period the patient was continuously treated with timolol, and epinephrine hydrochloride (Glaucon) drops were added at times when the IOP was high.

Patient 5 was a 61-year-old diabetic man with angle-recession glaucoma. He had been followed up for 7 years on medical therapy; his IOP ranged from 21 to 78 mm Hg. In February 1979 the patient underwent thermal sclerostomy and anterior lid sclerectomy. Within 1 month the IOP was again elevated to 40 mm Hg. Cyclocryotherapy brought the pressure below 30 mm Hg for approximately 1 year. Subsequent pressures were highly variable, between 4 and 38 mm Hg. In January 1981, 20 ciliary processes were treated with the laser. Postoperatively the IOP was elevated again to 32 mm Hg and a second treatment was performed. Since that time the IOP has ranged from 5 to 46 mm Hg (Fig. 6).

DISCUSSION

A review of the cases that have been reported to have failed helps us to understand better why others have been successful. When the ciliary epithelium is acutely injured, the production of aqueous is undoubtedly reduced. The ciliary epithelium has great regenerative capacity and secretion is soon resumed.[5] Histopathologic sections show that photocoagulation disturbs the circulation of blood in the ciliary body.[6] Hence a burn intense enough to coagulate the vessels leading to the ciliary processes would be more likely to give a prolonged effect. Another possibility may be that secondary inflammation of the ciliary body could be responsible for the postoperative lowering of IOP. After the initial injury, hypersecretion may occur secondary to vascular dilation. This effect may be moderated in the immediate posttreatment period by the hyposecretion resulting from the direct injury and inflammation that later subsides.

The potential complications of the procedure should be considered. All of the cases were done using topical anesthesia, and no patient reported excessive pain intraoperatively. Of the 25 eyes reported in the literature,[2-4] plus our 5 cases, several patients had a mild corneal punctuate epitheliopathy, which healed rapidly. Most patients had transient iridocyclitis that cleared within 1 week of treatment with the use of topical steroids. There were no reported complications secondary to stray burns striking the peripheral retina.

A review of the individual case reports shows that two of the patients (patients 1 and 2) had improvement in IOP control after treatment of the ciliary processes. Patient 1 required multiple treatments, but a gradual return of preoperative pressure elevation eventually required cyclocry-

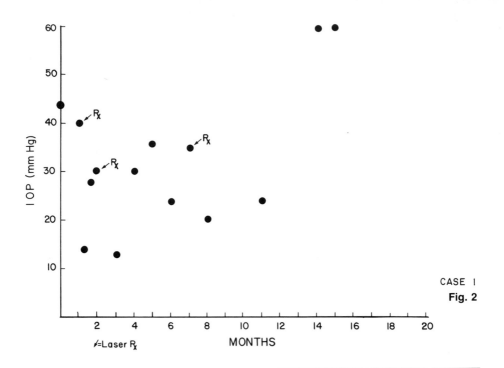

CASE I

Fig. 2

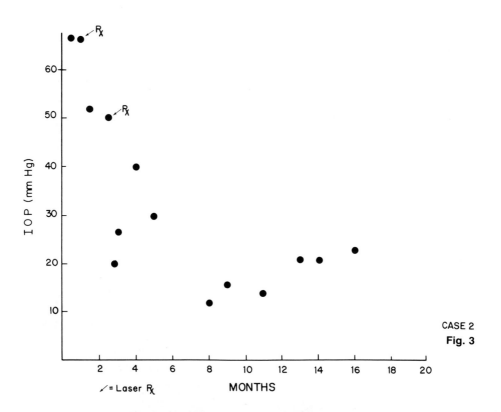

CASE 2

Fig. 3

Figures 2–6. Graphs of the IOP in Patients 1 to 5.

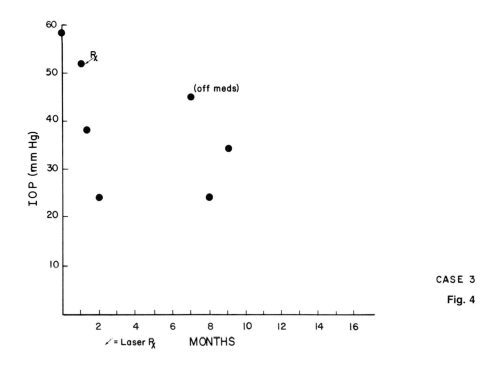

(off meds)

R_x

IOP (mm Hg)

MONTHS

/ = Laser R_x

CASE 3

Fig. 4

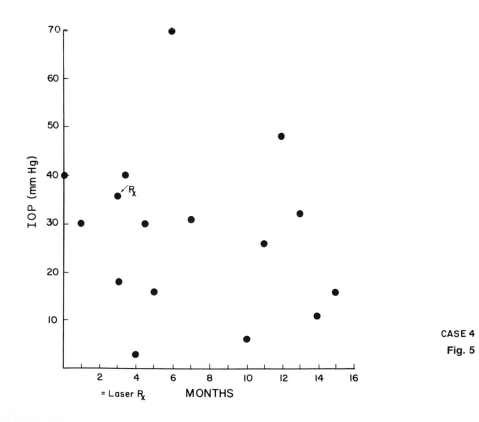

R_x

IOP (mm Hg)

MONTHS

= Laser R_x

CASE 4

Fig. 5

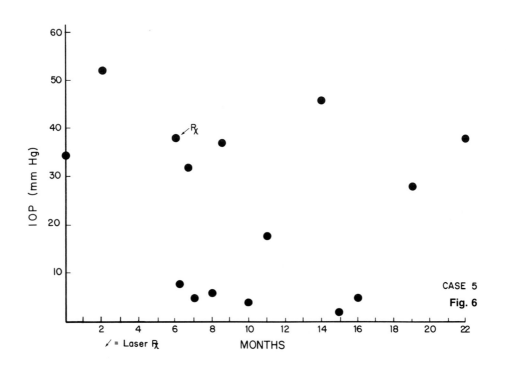

CASE 5

Fig. 6

otherapy. Patient 2 has had sustained decreased IOP since her second treatment. There are insufficient data to compare patient 3 with the others, although a moderately sustained reduction in IOP appears to have occurred. Patients 4 and 5 have had highly variable pressures preoperatively and postoperatively, making it difficult to assess any benefit from laser treatment.

It appears that there is potential benefit for some patients who undergo laser treatment to the ciliary processes. No definite conclusions can be made, however, to identify which patients may benefit from treatment.

REFERENCES

1. Lee P, Pomerantzeff O: Transpupillary cyclophotocoagulation of rabbit eyes. Am J Ophthalmol 71:911, 1971
2. Zimmerman TJ, Worthen DM, Wickham G: Argon laser photocoagulation of ciliary processes and pigmented pupillary membrane in man. Invest Ophthalmol 12:622, 1973
3. Merritt J: Transpupillary photocoagulation of the ciliary processes. Ann Ophthalmol 8:325, 1976

4. Lee P: Argon laser photocoagulation for the ciliary processes in cases of aphakic glaucoma. Arch Ophthalmol 97:2135, 1979
5. Worthen D: Laser treatment for glaucoma. Invest Ophthalmol 13:3, 1974
6. Weekers R, Laverge G, Watillon M, et al: Effects of photocoagulation of ciliary body upon ocular tension. Am J Ophthalmol 52:156, 1961

CHAPTER 8

Trabeculotomy

Alan L. Robin

In a minority of open-angle glaucoma patients maximal medical therapy fails to control satisfactorily the intraocular pressure (IOP), and some other forms of therapy must be employed. To date, the most successful therapy has been an external approach (filtration surgery), whereby a "safety valve" is formed beneath the conjunctiva. The newest type of filtering surgery, trabeculectomy, has been very successful with minimal complications. Since its inception over a decade ago, trabeculectomy has produced over an 80 percent success rate in patients with primary open-angle glaucoma. Approximately one-half of these successfully treated patients have been able to discontinue all antiglaucomatous medications. Despite this success, some unavoidable complications exist, including the need for hospitalization, a flat anterior chamber, cataract formation, wound leaks, endophthalmitis, and externalized anterior chambers. Trabeculectomies are also less likely to succeed in the eyes of young patients or in those that have undergone a previous operation.

To avoid some of these problems and to create a better procedure, researchers suggested using light energy to drill a hole through the internal trabecular meshwork and underlying sclera to the subconjunctival space. In 1973 Hager[1] first described the use of the laser to perform a trabeculo-electro puncture. Originally, he had excellent success: 19 of 28 patients had IOP decreases of 8 mm Hg. This technique became more well known when Krasnov[2] described the use of a Q-switched ruby laser to drill a hole in the trabecular meshwork to Schlemm's canal. The interpretation of his findings was relative. The procedure seemed to work

well. In fact, if the IOP rose postoperatively, the patient could be retreated with good success. However, these "laser" holes would repeatedly
close and require constant retreatment.

Because of the wider availability of argon lasers, many investigators
began to utilize this energy source to create an *ab interno* filtering procedure. Spitznas and Kreiger[3] tried using the argon laser in primates; however, all the holes they produced closed within the first 10 days. Fechner
and Teichmann[4] tried this procedure in humans, but had a dismal success
rate (7.9 percent).

Faced with these failures, Worthen and Wickman[5] abandoned the attempt to create a filtering hole with the argon laser. Instead, they treated the
angle circumferentially with 50-μ spot sizes and power settings that ranged
from 1 to 3 W. They reported excellent results in 24 human eyes, and
because of this treatment, surgery was avoided in these patients. When their
technique was presented at the annual meeting of the American Academy of
Ophthalmology, it was viewed as experimental and potentially dangerous.
About the same time, experiments in primates[6] showed that photocoagulation of the trabecular meshwork could produce glaucoma in monkeys.
However, this technique in primates used five times the amount of energy
that was used in the IOP-reducing technique of Worthen and Wickham.
This difference in energy possibly explains the conflicting results.

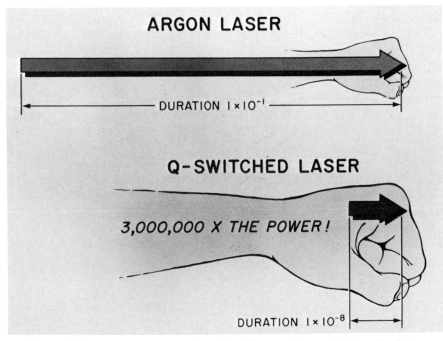

Figure 1. Schematic representation of the difference between the long duration,
low energy argon laser burn and the short duration high energy Q-switched laser
burn.

The cool reception of Worthen's and Wickham's[5] work caused a reluctance to continue this line of research. In 1978 Ticho and coworkers[7] again attempted experimental work using the argon laser to treat open-angle glaucoma. Using light and scanning electron microscopy, they demonstrated that this technique produced coagulative necrosis and complete closure of areas within the trabecular meshwork in 3 weeks and increased outflow for only 2 weeks.[7] Credit must be given to Wise and Witter[8] who popularized the technique of scattered angle treatment with the argon laser for open-angle glaucoma. They in fact demonstrated good IOP reduction in a 1-year follow-up. Additional reports confirming the success of the technique appeared in 1981.[9–11]

Some problems are inherent in the approach of Wise and Witter.[8] The pulse produced by the continuous-wave argon laser uses a low energy setting for a relatively long duration. Because of this, the argon laser's effect is mostly thermal. As this heat dissipates, there is the potential for extended burn size and extensive intraocular necrosis of tissue. An improvement would involve a technique utilizing pulses of short duration and very large amounts of power. This latter method would give the light energy a mechanical rather than a thermal effect and would enable a hole to be drilled rather than burned into the trabecular meshwork.

The Q-switched ruby laser can deliver this mechanical form of light energy. Q-switching releases light energy in short powerful pulses. Com-

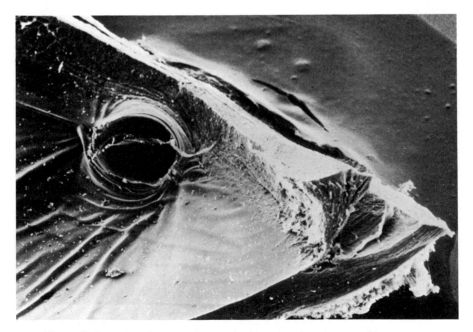

Figure 2. Scanning electron micrograph of a trabeculotomy created in a monkey trabecular meshwork with the Q-switched ruby laser.

CHAPTER 9

The Use of Neodymium:YAG Lasers in the Treatment of Glaucoma

Jacob T. Wilensky

As indicated in the introduction to this volume, there are a large number of different types of lasers that can be used for many different applications. In ophthalmology, we have used the argon lasers primarily and the ruby, krypton, and carbon dioxide lasers less often. With the exception of the ruby laser, all of these are continuous-wave lasers; that is, the laser light is steadily released over a determined period of time. The ruby is a pulsed laser that emits short bursts of energy, but it has a relatively long duration of action. All of these lasers work via a thermal mode. This means that the light energy from the laser is absorbed by the tissue, which is converted into heat, to create a burn that is utilized in treating the eye.

Recently, a new type of laser has been introduced to the ophthalmic community. This is the pulsed neodymium laser. The neodymium laser differs from the other lasers in that it produces a very short duration, high energy pulse of light that functions in a different manner from the low powered long duration instruments. The amount of energy contained in the pulses of light from the neodymium laser is so high that it actually causes changes in the structure of atoms that are hit by its light. This is called optical breakdown. Electrons can be torn away from the atoms in such a way that a mini-explosion occurs. This breakdown of the atoms creates a structure that is called plasma, which then blocks further transmission of light energy to a large extent. This mini-explosion not only disintegrates tissue at the focal point of the laser light but also creates a sonic wave, so that there is an extremely strong force that can mechanically disrupt tissue in addition to the disintegrating force of the light energy itself.

The currently available neodymium lasers utilize YAG crystals (yttrium, aluminum, and garnet) onto which the neodymium has been "doped." There are two different types of these lasers available. One group is mode-locked and uses a bleachable dye as a shutter for the release of the light energy. These lasers produce bursts of energy that are 30 to 100 picoseconds in duration (10^{-12} sec). The other neodymium:YAG lasers are Q-switched and utilize an electro-optical polarizing shutter to control the emissions. These lasers produce bursts of energy that are about 20 to 40 nanoseconds (10^{-9} sec) in duration. The neodymium lasers must be contrasted to the argon and krypton lasers, which commonly utilize a burn duration of 50 to 500 msec (10^{-3} sec). As the duration of the pulse is shortened, the power level is increased. Thus a 1 mJ Q-switched laser will generate 100,000 W and a mode-lock laser delivering 1 mJ will have a power level of 10 million W. Again, this must be contrasted with the average 1 W of power that is used with the argon laser.

Another feature that differentiates the neodymium lasers from the conventionally used ones is the wavelength of the light, which is 1064 nm. This means that the light produced by neodymium lasers is in the infrared range and is not visible to the human eye. This has two important meanings. Because of its wavelength, the absorption of the neodymium light is quite different in many tissues than is the light from the other lasers. There is relatively poor absorption by hemoglobin and only moderate absorption by melanin. This decreased absorption means that the neodymium light will penetrate deeper into tissue before it is absorbed. This is only true at lower power settings. When the power is above the level of optical breakdown, tissue absorption is no longer important.

Another significance of the infrared wavelength is that a separate system must be devised for aiming the laser. With argon and krypton, an attenuated beam of the regular laser light is used to focus the beam. With the neodymium:YAG lasers, an additional weak helium-neon laser that generates a red-colored light must be added to the system in a parfocal fashion. This light indicates where the unseen neodymium light is being focused. Many of the commercially available lasers use a rotating aiming beam with two spots 180 degrees apart. When they are brought into focus, they merge together to form a single spot. This allows a much finer focusing than can be done with just a single spot.

To date, the most common use of the neodymium laser in ophthalmology has been to open opacified posterior lens capsules following extracapsular cataract extraction usually associated with a posterior chamber intraocular lens implantation. Probably the next most common utilization has been to cut vitreous strands in anterior chambers.

As these instruments have become more available, the number of people exploring their possible use in various glaucoma treatments has increased. At the present time, the technique that has received the great-

est attention has been the performance of laser iridotomies. As previously mentioned in this volume, the power of argon lasers is somewhat marginal to create laser iridotomies. There are some patients in whom an iridotomy cannot be performed using an argon laser or in whom several treatment sessions are required to accomplish this task. Therefore, if the neodymium:YAG laser represents a superior technology, it will be rapidly accepted by many glaucoma therapists.

Initially, there was considerable fear as to whether laser iridotomies could be performed safely using a neodymium:YAG laser. The question was, in the process of tearing a hole in the iris, would one also make a hole in the anterior lens capsule? Clinical experience has indicated that it is quite possible to create an iridotomy safely without causing significant damage to the lens, provided that care and reasonable power settings are used. On the other hand, certain other problems have been encountered. There is a much greater tendency to cause bleeding, and even a significant hyphema, while performing a YAG iridotomy. The thermal lasers cauterize the iris vessels in the process of making the hole. The neodymium laser tears or shreds the iris, which may break the iris vessels.

The second problem is that there is no control over the size of the hole that is being produced. In my limited experience to date, I find that most iridotomies that I have created are definitely small. Once a hole is made, however, it cannot be enlarged (as can be done with the argon laser). There is a definite risk that if one is aiming around the edges and some of the energy goes through the iridotomy, an anterior capsulotomy of the lens may result. It is possible that as we gain more experience and learning we may be able to select optimum power settings for creating an iridotomy of the desired size.

Using a single pulse of a Q-switched neodymium:YAG laser, it appears that approximately 15 to 20 mJ are needed to create an iridotomy. A number of commercially available lasers have a feature that allows a burst of laser energy to contain from two to nine pulses. Each of the pulses is in the 20 to 40 nsec range of duration, with a separation between the pulses of about 20 msec. Thus, a burst containing nine of these pulses would last almost 0.2 second. It seems that with this very rapid train of pulses the tissues do not have a chance to recover from the first burst of energy before the next one arrives, which may cause greater damage than if similarly powered pulses were separated by longer durations. We have been using bursts that contain four pulses of energy with power settings between 4 and 8 mJ to create iridotomies. Usually, 6 mJ are adequate. A contact lens is used similar to the Abraham iridotomy lens but designed for neodymium lasers.

To deal with the problem of bleeding, some investigators have recommended pretreating the iris with thermal mode neodymium:YAG, as can be performed with the Lasag instrument, or argon burns from the lasers that have combined argon and neodymium capabilities. To me, this

does not make a great deal of sense. If one is going to treat with the argon, then there is no need for the neodymium. Moreover, the pretreatment will release a certain amount of pigment and debris into the aqueous that will decrease the effectiveness of the subsequent Q-switched neodymium pulses to penetrate the iris. On the other hand, if the argon fails to penetrate, then obviously it would make very good sense to aim the neodymium light at the center of the previously treated area.

What then would be the indications for YAG iridotomy at the present time? My own feeling is that there may be two main indications. The first would be the situation just mentioned, in which an attempt made with an argon laser has been unsuccessful. In our limited experience to date, we have had no difficulty penetrating irides with the neodymium:YAG laser that have been resistant to penetration with the argon laser. The second indication, I believe, would be for the patient who has a great deal of difficulty holding still at the laser. This would include patients with a tremor, as those with parkinsonism, or those who cooperate poorly. In the latter situation, only one or two laser pulses are delivered to the eye in contrast to the dozens or even hundreds of burns that are generally required with the argon technique. A third potential indication might be a situation in which it is clinically necessary to create an iridotomy immediately. This would be in an emergency situation in which the patient has an acute angle closure that needs to be broken immediately. Since argon treatment does not always work in this situation, one could argue for using the YAG laser. Because of my inexperience in this area, I do not know whether the neodymium laser will be any more efficient in eyes with edematous corneas resulting from elevated pressure or with significant anterior chamber reaction.

Another area of use of the neodymium:YAG laser for glaucoma that has been investigated to a limited extent is in reopening nonfunctioning filter sites. A few reports have described the successful restoration of filtration in which the internal ostium of a trabeculectomy opening has been plugged either by some type of membrane or by vitreous.[1] Several attempts have also been made to see if a hole could actually be drilled through to the subconjunctival space. There have been no reports of success so far. It should be pointed out that unless there is some potential subconjunctival space present for the aqueous to drain into, simply making a channel from the anterior chamber through the sclera probably will not have much, if any, beneficial effect. Sometimes, however, there is a nonfunctioning filtering bleb that is present because the bleb has become walled off by a capsule of Tenon's tissue. If this space could be entered with the laser, then conceivably filtration might be restored.

In a somewhat analogous manner, Fankhauser[2] has reported the ability to create channels from the anterior chamber into the suprachoroidal space by making holes through the scleral spur with his neodymium laser. Although these holes remained patent for a prolonged period of time,

they apparently did not have any significant pressure lowering effect on the patient's eye.

Fankhauser[2] has also investigated using the neodymium laser in the thermal mode to perform laser trabeculoplasty in a number of patients. He claims that the clinical results that he obtained using this technique were comparable to the ones that he has achieved using the standard argon laser technique. Thus far, there is no evidence to suggest any advantages to the neodymium laser.

An additional potential use of the neodymium:YAG laser that has been mentioned but has not yet really been explored clinically is in photocoagulation of the ciliary processes. This can be accomplished in two different manners. The first is transscleral photocoagulation of the ciliary body. As mentioned in an earlier chapter, Beckman has used a pulsed ruby laser to create burns in the ciliary body to lower the intraocular pressure in patients with glaucoma. Because of the laser's ability to penetrate tissue, it is quite reasonable to think that the same effect could be accomplished using the thermal mode of the neodymium:YAG laser. We have, in fact, conducted some experiments in rabbits that have confirmed that lesions can be created in the ciliary body by this technique. We have not yet tested this method in humans, so we cannot say whether it will be a useful clinical tool or not.

A second way in which the laser might be used to treat the ciliary processes would be transpupillary photocoagulation of the ciliary processes. As was previously mentioned in this volume, there has been some experience with the use of transpupillary argon laser photocoagulation of the ciliary processes, but the reported results are somewhat mixed, and this technique has not gained widespread acceptance. Because the neodymium light is only moderately absorbed by melanin, there is a theoretic expectation that more of the energy might penetrate deeper into the ciliary process and therefore cause more damage in the core of the process instead of just to the pigment epithelium. This in turn might lead to more significant and/or prolonged damage than the argon laser burns. So far, there have been no reports of using the neodymium:YAG laser for this purpose. Obviously, considerable experimentation will be necessary to determine the optimum parameters for this type of treatment before one can then evaluate the clinical usefulness of this treatment.

In summary, the use of neodymium:YAG lasers is still in its infancy. It does appear that they will have a definite application in the treatment of glaucoma patients, but with the possible exception of laser iridotomy, it is much too early to determine just how they will be employed. In all of these applications, including iridotomy, we still have much to learn concerning the treatment parameters and much experience will be required before guidelines for the use of the neodymium lasers can be established.

REFERENCES

1. Cohn HC, Aron-Rosa D: Re-opening blocked trabeculectomy sites with the YAG lasers. Am J Ophthalmol 95:293, 1983
2. Fankhauser F: The Q-switched laser: Principles and clinical results. In Trokel SL (ed): YAG Laser Ophthalmic Microsurgery. Norwalk, Conn., Appleton-Century-Crofts, 1983, pp 101–146

Index

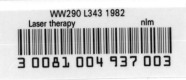